# Discover the
# GREEK
# ISLANDS

## COMPLETE TOURIST GUIDE

### 70 DETAILED MAPS
### 380 COLOUR PHOTOS

editions HAÏTALIS

Copyright © 2004, Editions Haitali, 13, Astrous St., 13121 Athens, Tel:2105766883 - Fax: 2105729985

# Contents

# INTRODUCTION

Scattered small pieces of paradise, floating on crystal waters, some windswept, others wrapped up in the warm embrace of the sun. Stone bridges emerging from the sea, uniting the mainland with the horizon, allowing us to move from east to west and from north to south, with the whole world congregating on their fertile soil, becoming one, retaining the feeling that the joy of creation has not yet been lost.

One these dry rocks spewed out by volcanoes, made of lava and light, low white houses protrude, warm nests for the locals and for passers by, foreigners, who all at once become both friend and relative. White houses with their whitewashed yards, clean, purified and yet flooded with colour from the geraniums and basil plants. The air is heavy with jasmine whose scent reaches all the way down to the shore where it mingles with the sea air, the two scents struggling to see which will win, which will captivate us. We float freely in the sea, letting our bodies unwind, letting our bodies be carried hither and yonder by the gently lapping of the translucent waters, let the burning sun fry our wounds, heal us, save us. And the boats, green and brown, purple and red, sway gently with their mermaid figures on their sterns and Poseidon painted on their sails to ameliorate the god of the sea into calming the storms with his trident, allowing us to sail to other quiet shores.

Once the ship docks at the port, the travellers pour forth onto the jetty like busy bees, eager to quench their hunger and thirst on the sweet fruits of the land. The islands come alive, sigh in relief, and gather up reserves for the lonely winter evenings. The shops fling open their

doors, tables in the taverns are laid, the wine of Dionysus flows, to please the foreigners and make them forget their concerns for a while; to sing along with guitars and bouzoukis, to dance away their melancholy, to talk, to meet others, to desire, to fall in love. A walk along the sandy beach at night, in the light of the full moon, with the waves gently breaking in the silent air and the music of some lyre players resounding from afar. Only to find us at dawn in the streets, a bustling fair of sounds and colours…

Shortly before dawn the baker finishes baking his bread and the air fills with its smell, the last pleasure of the night, the first of the day. Further on is the grocer with his refreshing fruit and juicy, red tomatoes, with the flavour of ambrosia, with a taste like one we have never tasted before; it is as if we have been invited by the gods to this rich meal of theirs, and in comes Athena with an olive branch, to offer us her tasty gifts, so that we lack in nothing these days.

The favoured of the moon, the beloved of the gods… because the gods have not given up. They have defeated time and are still alive. They smile on us, wink cunningly at us, when we take a rest in one of their temples, when we hear our voice echo in their theatres, when we secretly stroke the marble hair of an Olympian victor, when a lithe woman, Aphrodite, slowly emerging from the foam of the waves, enchants us. But the blond child descending from on high is not the winged Eros. He is an angel, our angel, some prophet from our god. He crosses the threshold of a humble church and we follow him. A candle lit before the icon, the slow burning ex voto, lavender, incense and the chanter to calm our soul until the Virgin takes the hand of Aphrodite and all goddesses in this world. They leave the churches and start dancing among the forest foliage, on the high mountains, on the edge of cliffs, where the pine bends down to stroke the sea, to kiss it reverentially.

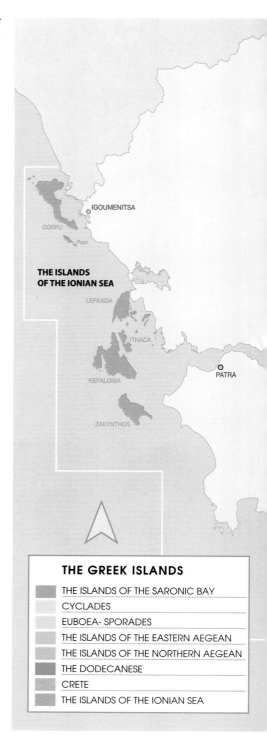

**THE ISLANDS OF THE IONIAN SEA**

IGOUMENITSA

CORFU

Paxi

LEFKADA

ITHACA

KEFALONIA

PATRA

ZAKYNTHOS

**THE GREEK ISLANDS**

THE ISLANDS OF THE SARONIC BAY
CYCLADES
EUBOEA- SPORADES
THE ISLANDS OF THE EASTERN AEGEAN
THE ISLANDS OF THE NORTHERN AEGEAN
THE DODECANESE
CRETE
THE ISLANDS OF THE IONIAN SEA

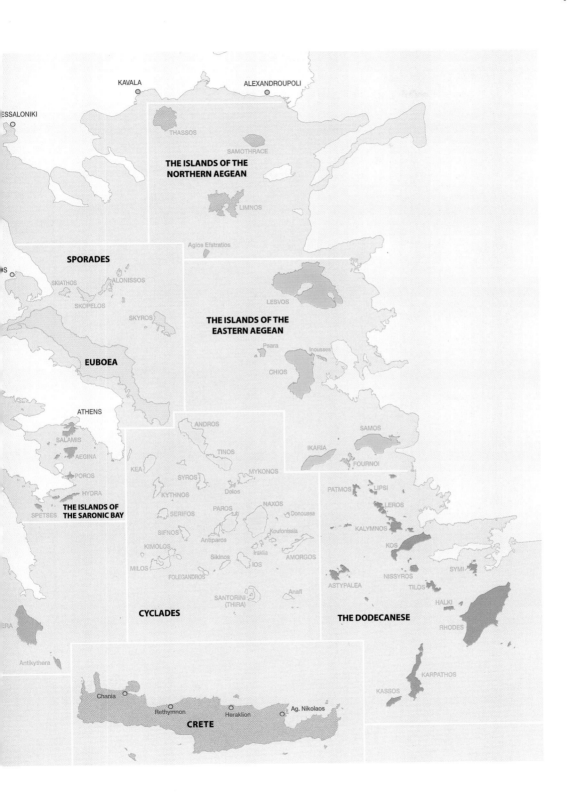

KAVALA
ALEXANDROUPOLI
ESSALONIKI

THASSOS
SAMOTHRACE

**THE ISLANDS OF THE
NORTHERN AEGEAN**

LIMNOS

Agios Efstratios

**SPORADES**

S

SKIATHOS          ALONISSOS

SKOPELOS

SKYROS

LESVOS

**THE ISLANDS OF THE
EASTERN AEGEAN**

**EUBOEA**

Psara          Inousses

CHIOS

ATHENS

ANDROS

SALAMIS

TINOS

SAMOS

AEGINA

KEA          MYKONOS

IKARIA

POROS

SYROS          Delos

FOURNOI

HYDRA

KYTHNOS

PATMOS          LIPSI

**THE ISLANDS OF
THE SARONIC BAY**

SPETSES          SERIFOS

PAROS

NAXOS          Donoussa

LEROS

SIFNOS          Antiparos

Koufonissia

KALYMNOS

KIMOLOS          Sikinos          Iraklia

KOS

MILOS          IOS          AMORGOS

NISSYROS          SYMI

FOLEGANDROS

ASTYPALEA          TILOS

SANTORINI
(THIRA)          Anafi

HALKI

**CYCLADES**

**THE DODECANESE**

RHODES

ERA

Antikythera

KARPATHOS

KASSOS

Chania

Rethymnon          Heraklion          Ag. Nikolaos

**CRETE**

The Greek islands were always a source of inspiration for artists from all over the world. The beauty of their landscape remains intact to this day despite the changes wrought by time. No one will be unmoved by the picturesque quality of the island villages, the endless stretch of sea surrounding them, the deep red hue of the sunset and the sense of unconcern, of joy one can feel on those islands even if only for a few days.

The singularity of the Greek archipelago is mainly owed to its geographical setting. In no other spot of the European continent

is the land so fragmented into so many small pieces scattered in the sea. Of the 500 or so larger and smaller islands, some 227 are inhabited. Their combined area is 25,166.24 square kilometres and their total population amounts to 1,500,000. Spread out from the Ionian to the Aegean Sea, their southern boundary is Crete, the fifth largest island in the Mediterranean.

The result of volcanic eruptions or massive seismic upheavals, each island is endowed with a beauty of its own. Sheer cliffs alternate with sheltered beaches, some with black sand – in startling con-

trast to the green hills, the blue sea and the dazzling white houses.

All the islands have also had a turbulent history. They were initially settled by tribes from every corner of the Mediterranean in prehistoric times and brilliant civilizations developed on many of them. The island-museum of Delos; the half-finished, abandoned Kouroi of Naxos; the extraordinary Minoan palaces in Crete; the medieval grandeur of Rhodes and Kos; all the vestiges of everyday life in the ancient world still visible in the mute ruins cannot fail to move even the most unhistorical-minded visitor.

The island clusters of Greece, thanks to their geographical location and their natural endowments, were the "bone of contention" for numerous ambitious conquerors.

Their inhabitants, motivated by the practical need for self-protection, created an original architectural style distinguished by plasticity of form and economy of line. Small white houses with brightly painted windows and doors, picturesque churches scattered throughout, winding flag stoned lanes were all made with unsurpassed art and care by simple islanders.

In their attempt to preserve their Greek

identity intact, the islanders kept to their old traditions and many still live according to their established ways and customs. All will be intrigued by the living folk art museum that is the island of Karpathos and the women in traditional costumes, the sponge fisherman of the Dodecanese, the island craftsmen still making their caiques according to the age-old methods of their forefathers. And who could fail to be impressed by the unbelievable stories told by the old people of Symi and Mytilini about their patron saints.

This book gives an outline of the history of each island and a brief description of its life today, but its main aim is to show that there is something in Greece for everyone – for the history enthusiast who ignores the contemporary scene, for the tourist who seeks the solace of the sun and sea, for the person in quest of quiet or sophisticated pleasures. The beauty of the scenery, the illustrious history, the remnants of a radiant civilization -all justify the international reputation of the islands as well as the nostalgia that overcomes the traveller at the end of his sojourn.

# THE ISLANDS OF THE
# SARONIC BAY

The islands of the Saronic Bay occupy the maritime area between the southwestern shores of Attica and the northeastern shores of the Peloponnese. The closest islands to Attica are Salamina and Aegina while close to the Peloponnese lie Poros, Hydra and Spetses. There are also numerous smaller islands in the Saronic Bay such as the verdant Angistri, which lies to the west of Aegina.

Thanks to their short distance from Athens, the islands of the Saronic Bay are a pole of attraction for all those who want to escape from the clamour of the big city. Residents of the capital frequently visit these islands on weekends, escaping for a while from their daily concerns. Tourists too who travel to Athens – particularly those who have a little time at their disposal – rarely resist the temptation for a quick tour around the Saronic Bay enabling them to acquire a taste of island Greece without the hassle of a long trip, not just because these islands lie only a short distance from the port of Piraeus but also due to the good weather conditions which normally prevail at sea in the Saronic Bay.

The five largest islands in the Saronic Bay were inhabited from very early on. On almost all, remains of settlements from the prehistoric period have been found while their distant past is illuminated by a series of myths which interpret their names and provide important information about their first inhabitants. During the classical period their history was associated in large part with the historical development of nearby Athens. When Athens was at the pinnacle of its

glory, Aegina was an important centre of worship since it was home to the temple of Aphaia (a divinity with pre-Hellenic roots) which was visited by the faithful from all over Greece. At the same time, an important sanctuary had also been established on Poros dedicated to the god Poseidon. The famed rhetorician Demosthenes sought refuge and ended his days there in 332 BC. On the other hand Salamina has gone down in history because of the famed naval battle of Salamis that took place during the Persian Wars and was of decisive importance for the victory of the Greeks over the Persians. Moreover, it was also the birthplace of the great tragic poet Euripides.

In more recent times, when Greece was seized by the Turks in 1453 certain of the islands in the Saronic Bay managed to flourish such as Hydra and Spetses, which were placed under a semi-autonomous regime within the boundaries of the Ottoman Empire. During the Greek Revolution against the Turks in 1821, the contribution of these islands to the Greek struggle was important thanks to their naval forces. Following liberation, Aegina was the first capital of the newly formed Greek State from 1828 to 1829 with Athens finally being chosen as capital in 1834.

The islands of the Saronic Bay have developed rapidly since Greece began to emerge as an important tourist destination, with a

continuous flow of visitors from all over the world. To this day they owe their prosperity primarily to tourism. Aegina is one of the islands with the largest tourist flows in the entire country. Their success in this sector has not been left to chance and is certainly not due solely to their close proximity to mainland Greece. They lack nothing in comparison with the other islands of the Aegean. They are sun-drenched, have retained their traditional character, while each one has its own timbre and has something different to offer. For example, Spetses, an island decked in green, stands out for its luxury summer villas, its

squares, its pebbled streets and the monuments to its glorious past from the time of Turkish rule. Hydra, dry yet imposing and cosmopolitan, with a completely personal character, is one of the officially recognized traditional villages of Greece. There are no cars anywhere on the island while the refined green hue of the stone used in the old mansions which are still standing today, comes into strong contrast with the vibrant crowds wandering through the town's winding lanes.

Forest-covered Poros leaves one speechless with its picturesque aspect and its views to Galatas on the shores of the Peloponnese.

Aegina gives visitors a sense of calm despite the high tourist influxes. Its picturesque, yet bustling, port is always full of small fishing boats while, if one is interested in shopping, there are the famed ceramics made with skill by local residents. One cannot leave the island without visiting the temple of Aphaia, one of the best-preserved temples in Greece. Salamina for its part, although lying closer than the other islands to the industrial zone surrounding the capital, has much to recompense the visitor in terms of the sense of calm on its isolated bays, verdant hill sides and in its seaside villages.

# Salamis

**HISTORY:** The island is said to have taken its name from the nymph Salamis. It played a major role in ancient history thanks to its position in the gulf of Elefsis.

According to Homer, its men took part in the Trojan War. Later it became the apple of discord between Athens and Megara. But the most important event to which it contributed was the naval battle fought in 480 BC between the Greeks and the Persians, forever remembered as the Naval Battle of Salamis.

**SIGHTSEEING:** Excavations have revealed a Mycenaean necropolis and ruined city walls. A rounded hill on the Kynosoura peninsula is thought to be the tomb of the Greeks who fell in the naval battle in 480 BC. Finds unearthed in the area are on display in the island's archaeological museum. The village of Moulki is held to be the birthplace of the legendary hero Ajax.

*Area:* 95 sq. km. **Population:** 28,574
*Capital:* Salamis (Salamina) or Koulouri
*How to get there:* By boat from Piraeus or Perama

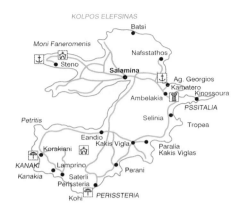

Salamis is also filled with Byzantine monuments. The oldest are the Faneromeni convent, first constructed in the 11th century, the church of Agios Ioannis Kalyvitis dating from the 12th-13th century, and the much later monastery of Agios Nikolaos (18th c.). The island lends itself to relaxing holidays, in its small, delightful villages (Ambelakia, Selinia) and on its beautiful beaches to the southwest (Kanakia, Kalones).

# Aegina

**HISTORY:** The island, which took its name from the nymph Aegina, has been inhabited since the third millennium BC. The first Greek settlers arrived around 2000 BC; from the beginning they were merchants and seafarers. The Aeginetans minted the first coinage known on the European continent in the 7th century BC. They took part in the Persian Wars, but later fell under Athenian sway and suffered a decline. During the Hellenistic period, the Romans sold the island to Attalos, king of Pergamon. Barbarossa devastated Aegina in 1537; it was repopulated by Albanians during the Turkish Occupation. The island provided sanctuary to many Revolutionary heroes in 1821. When Kapodistrias became Greece's first governor, Aegina became the first capital of modern Greece, albeit for only one year. In that short time, the island saw the founding of the Military Academy, the

*Area: 85 sq. km. Population: 11,167 Capital: Aegina*
*How to get there: By boat, ferryboat and Flying Dolphin from*
*Piraeus, the Peloponnese and neighbouring islands*

National Printing Press, the National Bank and first currency of the new country.

**SIGHTSEEING:** In antiquity the island was renowned for its sculpture and pottery and for the temple of Aphaia, one of the most important of ancient times. This temple, later identified with the worship of Athena, lies above the resort of Agia Marina. The pediments with their exquisite sculptures were

carried off in 1813 by Prince Ludwig of Bavaria and can now be seen in the Munich Museum of Sculpture. Other antiquities include the temple of Apollo-Poseidon, the sanctuary of Zeus Hellanios, etc. Finds from these sites are exhibited at the museum in the capital.

Since the Byzantine era the island has been proud of its churches – Agios Theodoroi (1282) with excellent frescoes – and monasteries – Agia Aikaterina and Agios Nektarios, which attract thousands of pilgrims each year. Covering a hillside outside town, there is the old Byzantine capital of the island, Palaiohora.

Aegina, which has seen tremendous tourist development in recent years, has splendid beaches and charming fishing villages (Perdika, Souvala, Kolona). It is also linked daily with the nearby islet of Angistri, which attracts numerous visitors, especially in summer.

# Poros

**HISTORY:** Poros is really two islands united by a narrow strip of land. In ancient times, these two parts were known as Sphairia and Kalavria. In the 7th century, Kalavria, the legendary birthplace of Theseus, was the centre of a league of seven cities. The league's religious headquarters was the important temple of Poseidon. During the Byzantine era, Poros – like most of the islands – was frequently raided by pirates, and fell into decline. It sprang to life at the start of the Revolution and took an active part in it. A few years later (1830) Poros became the site of the first Greek naval base.

**SIGHTSEEING:** Today all that remains of the island's prominence and its sanctuary of Poseidon are references by historians of the time. Excavations conducted in 1894 by Swedish archaeologists brought to light only a few remains of the temple, near the Bay of Vayionia, in

*Area:* 23 sq. km. - *Population:* 3,929 - *Capital:* Poros
*How to get there:* By boat, or Flying Dolphin from Piraeus
(Zea), Hydra, Spetses and the Peloponnese

the north of the island. The temple is said to
have sheltered the ancient orator Demosthenes until his suicide. The scant finds from the
excavations can be seen in the local museum.
The Monastery of Zoodochos Pighi lies south
of the ancient temple.

Poros delights the eye with its verdant landscape and lovely beaches. The capital is built
in the island style, with its two-storey houses and narrow whitewashed lanes densely

covering a low hill. One of the most beautiful areas on the island is its western coast,
the Megalo Neorio. Little boats from Poros
constantly make the short crossing to Gala-
ta on the mainland, from where one can visit the archaeological sites of the Argolid,
the beaches at Alyki and the famous Lemon
Forest. Equally deserving attention, however, are the island beaches of Askeli and
Monastiri.

# Hydra

**HISTORY:** The island was known as Hydra in antiquity (from the 6th c. BC) as well as in the few Greek medieval sources in which it is mentioned. It has been inhabited since the distant past, as shown by the ruins of the Mycenaean settlement discovered to the west of the port. First subject to Mycenae, it later passed to Hermione, which sold the island to Samians. During the Middle Ages, the island appears to have been deserted or sparsely populated by shepherds. The first colonists arrived in the 15th century with the Turkish expansion into the Peloponnese. Hydra flourished during the 17th and 18th centuries; it was then that the Hydrians established their magnificent merchant fleet and the island really progressed. Later this fleet offered its services to the struggle for independence and distinguished itself in the Revolution. Most of the famous admirals and sea captains of this

*Area: 64 sq. km. Population: 2,723 Capital: Hydra*
*How to get there: By boat, ferryboat and Flying Dolphin from*
*Piraeus (Zea), Aegina, Methana, Poros, Spetses, Ermioni*

era came from Hydra. The naval tradition continues up to the present with its Merchant Marine Academy.

**SIGHTSEEING:** Hydra is the most cosmopolitan of the Saronic islands. Its capital is among the most unusual and architecturally interesting in Greece. The town has spread over the steep slopes of the hills surrounding the port, in a manner very similar to an ancient theatre

with the harbour taking the place of the orchestra. It grew up around the Monastery of Assumption, founded in 1641. Of special note are the old mansions, two- or three-storey stone edifices with symmetrically placed openings. The Tombazi mansion houses a department of the School of Fine Arts, while the museum's archives are filled with material from the Revolution. Besides the narrow, stepped alleyways, another architectural feature peculiar to Hydra is the deep colours of its houses, which are often the same as those decorating the caiques belonging to their owners. Apart from the Cathedral, worth visiting are the monasteries of Agia Triada, Agios Nikolaos, Agia Matrona and Prophitis Ilias. The monastery of the Assumption, Zourva, lies on the northeast coast of the island. On its south flank is the Byzantine city, near the hamlet of Episkopi.

There are few beaches, but one can swim at Mandraki, Kaminia, Vlychos and Molos. The town offers a number of hotels (many of them converted mansions), rooms in private houses and apartments.

# Spetses

**HISTORY:** Known to the ancients as Pityoussa, the island was first inhabited in the Bronze Age (2500-2000 BC). Near the church of Agia Marina, excavations have unearthed traces of Roman and early Christian buildings. It seems that the fear of pirates prevented the establishment of any organized settlement until the 17th century. After that time, people from the surrounding areas began to take up residence there. They joined the existing Albanian population moved there during the 15th century and settled themselves at the fortified location called Kastelli.

The Spetsiots engaged in commerce and shipping and soon developed into admirable seamen; their navy played a decisive role in the War of Independence. The figure of Laskarina Bouboulina, the lady admiral, became a legend; her casket is on display in the local museum.

*Area: 22 sq. km. **Population:** 3,700 **Capital:** Spetses **How to get there:** By boat, ferryboat and Flying Dolphin from Piraeus (Zea), the other Saronic islands and various areas of the Peloponnese*

**SIGHTSEEING:** The landmarks in Spetses are mainly of Byzantine and folkloric interest. Of particular interest are the churches of Agios Nikolaos, Agion Panton, the Assumption and the Anargyrion School.

The museum is housed in the Hatziyianni Mexis mansion and includes traditional arts and crafts and mementos from the Revolution. The small bustling harbour, Dappia, boasts six cannons dating from the War of Indepen-

dence. Around the harbour, cafes, restaurants and pastry shops provide much of the island's social life, which is very lively, particularly in summer.

Caiques leave from Dappia for the beautiful bays and coves surrounding the island – Agios Georgios, Agia Paraskevi, Vrellos, Xylokeriza, Agia Marina, for the precipitous northwest coast and Petrokaravo islet, the bay of Agioi Anargyroi and the Bekiri cave. Visitors can also join excursions to the archaeological sites and beaches of Argolid. Southeast of Spetses lies another wooded island, Spetsopoula, owned by the ship owner Niarchos.

# CYCLADES

The Cyclades are a group of islands in the Aegean which are in effect the mountain peaks of the sunken continent of Aegeis. They consist of two approximately parallel lines of islands (Andros, Tinos, Mykonos, Delos and Rhenia; Kea, Kythnos, Serifos and Sifnos) at the centre of which lie Syros and Yaros, with a third line across the southern extremity of the first two (Naxos, Paros and Antiparos). The islands of Milos, Folegandros, Kimolos, Sikinos, Ios, Amorgos, Anafi, Thira (Santorini) and Makronisos also belong, administratively, to the Cyclades. The name 'Cyclades' dates back to ancient times, and stems from the fact that all the islands form a kind of circle around Delos, the sacred island of the ancient Greeks. The Cyclades are mountainous, barren islands, but their unique architectural character has contributed much to the image which most foreigners have of Greece. The low, whitewashed houses with their courtyards full of fragrant flowers, the narrow cobbled lanes, the bare mountains leading down to sandy beaches, the calm sea and the hot summer sun - these are the components of a dream which leaves none of the world's travellers unaffected.

As a result of their geographical position, the Cyclades have long been a bridge between East and West, and they have played an important part in the history of the Greek world. Traces of habitation in the Neolithic period have come to light on Kea, Naxos and Antiparos (Salangos), and in the Early Bronze Age a unique civilisation - today called 'Cycladic' - formed in the islands (3rd millennium BC). Our knowledge of the Cycladic civilisation stems from the numerous sites which archaeologists have discovered in the islands. In

those early times, the islanders were farmers, shepherds, fishermen or merchants trading in the valuable goods of the age: obsidian from Milos, copper from Serifos and Sifnos, marble from Paros and Naxos. The islanders of the Cyclades were skilled in the arts and crafts, and particularly in pottery, sculpture and metal-working. The most representative examples of Cycladic art are the marble statuettes found in the area, and now to be seen in most Greek museums and in many collections in other countries. The statuettes depict nude female figures, usually upright but occasionally seated, which impress the viewer with their abstractive, plain and severe proportions. These features remained consistent throughout the Bronze Age, but in the later subdivisions of the period there are clear influences from Minoan Crete, which had begun to penetrate and dominate the Aegean. The most important settlement of the Late Bronze Age was found at Akrotiri on Thera. In the historical period, most of the Cycladic islands were colonised by Ionians, although some of them - such as Thera and Milos - were Doric colonies. After the late ninth century BC,

Delos, the island where Apollo was born, became a fully-fledged sanctuary to the god and evolved into a religious centre of importance for the entire Greek world. The growth of shipping and trade as early as the Archaic period, and contacts with lands further to the east through the various colonies, fostered the development of the Cyclades. In the seventh century BC, and particularly in the sixth, Cycladic art made important steps forward under the influence of nearby Ionia. In the early fifth century, the islands came under Persian control, and were liberated after 480 BC, when they joined the Athenian League. When the Peloponnesian War was over, Sparta became the dominant power, and it was not until 375 BC that the Cyclades came back into the Athenian sphere of influence. In 363 BC they were occupied by Epaminondas of Thebes for a short period, and in 338 BC the Macedonians took over. Under the Romans, the islands suffered at the hands of various barbarians, and in Byzantine times they underwent the depredations of the Slavs and the Saracens. After 1204, they were occupied by Franks, Venetians and Turks.

Although there is a general uniformity about the Cyclades today, each island has its own distinctive personality, and each has something unique to offer the visitor.»

On Kea or Tzia it is worth one's while visiting the ruins of the prehistoric settlement of Ayia Irini. Kynthos is ideal for quiet holidays as is Serifos, whose island capital is marked by its ruined Venetian fortress. On Sifnos the island capital, Apollonia, built amphitheatre-like, is impressive as are its numerous monasteries and picturesque villages.

Volcanic Milos, rich even today in mineral ores, was the only place in Greece in prehistoric times where obsidian was mined. Kimolos, Folegandros and Sikinos are small forgotten corners of paradise while Ios is extremely popular with tourists these days.

Santorini (or Thira) provides unrivalled views since it rises from the sea like a precipitous rock surrounded by the volcanic islets of Thirasia, Aspronisi and Nea and Palea Kammeni. The capital (Fira), clinging to the grey rocks, is one of the most cosmopolitan places in the Mediterranean. Of particular interest is the traditional architecture of Oia in the north of the island. To the south lie the ruins of the prehistoric settlement of Akrotiri. It is the best-preserved prehistoric settlement in the Aegean. This is due to the eruption of Santorini's volcano around 1500 BC which covered the place in a thick layer of ash, preserving it untouched over the centuries.

Close to Santorini is the small, yet idyllic, island of Anafi and to the north is Amorgos, one of the most typical Cycladic islands. The Venetian fortress in the island's capital and the monastery of Hozoviotissa, carved into

the rock, are impressive sights on Amorgos.

Naxos is the largest and most fertile of the Cycladic islands. With a rich past, today it is home to remarkable monuments from antiquity. The most impressive is the enormous gateway from the Ionic temple of Apollo at Palatia (530 BC) while the area around the Venetian fortress in the island's capital is particularly picturesque. Numerous Byzantine churches decorated with remarkable wall paintings have survived in an excellent state of repair on Naxos.

Paros presents similar archaeological interest. In the island capital of Parikia the remains of a Cycladic period village were found at the site of the ancient acropolis. Of particular interest is the medieval castle of Parikia built of ancient building materials as well as the Katapoliani Church. Close to Paros lies Antiparos, with which it was once united in prehistoric times. On the islet of Saliangos, which lies between the two islands, the remains of an important Neolithic settlement have been unearthed.

Mykonos, a typical Cycladic island, has a huge influx of tourists. Its capital crowned with picturesque windmills has a cosmopolitan feel. At the edge of the port lies the church of Paraportiani, the most important of the 400 or so adorning the island. Small boats bring visitors to the now uninhabited island of Delos, where one can see the ruins of the temple of Apollo which occupy an extensive archaeological site. There is an

archaeological museum on the island with portable finds from the area.

Picturesque Syros is the capital of the Prefecture of the Cyclades. Ermoupolis, the island's capital, is built amphitheatre-like on two hills, and stands out for its neoclassic buildings from the time when it was a thriving naval and small industrial centre.

Tinos is famed for the church of the Virgin of the Annunciation (Evangelistria) which was erected in 1823 to house the miraculous icon of the Virgin and is today a popular pilgrimage destination. The residents of Tinos are well known for their skill with marble while the renowned pigeon cotes scattered across the island are an important attraction.

Andros was once known as Hydrousa

thanks to its spa springs. The capital is built on the site of a medieval city and the remains of a Venetian fortress have survived. Portable finds are housed in a state-of-the-art archaeological museum in the island's capital. Of particular interest is the Museum of Modern Art which houses periodic exhibitions during summertime.

# Kea

**HISTORY:** The island was inhabited during the Neolithic era and took its name from the mythical hero Keos. Around the beginning of the first millennium the Ionians established colonies there and founded four independent cities –Ioulis, Karthaia, Poieessa, Korissia – all of which flourished. Later Kea became a member of the Athenian Confederacy and took part in the Persian Wars. Its decline began with the Roman conquest. During the Crusades and afterwards it was one of Venice's Aegean possessions. Like the other islands it was laid waste by Barbarossa in 1537 and subsequently fell to the Turks. In 1781 the Revolutionary hero Lambros Katsonis made Kea his base of operations.

**SIGHTSEEING:** Little remains of the four ancient cities. Excavations of the American School at Agia Irini have unearthed an important Bronze Age settlement, whose finds are on display in the Hora museum. In the capital, built on a hillside on the site of ancient Ioulis,

*Area:* 131 sq. km. *Population:* 1,618 *Capital:* Ioulis (Hora)
*Port:* Koryssia (Livadi) *How to get there:* By daily boat from
Lavrion and in summer weekly boats from Piraeus and Kythnos

the traditional Cycladic architecture is pre-served intact.

Near the town there are remains of a Venetian castle. To the northeast, carved out of rock, is the colossal "Lion of Kea", the work of an Ionian sculptor of the 7th century BC. Also worth noting are the Byzantine monasteries Agia Philothei (16th c.) and Panayia Kastriani. The island is dotted with lovely coves and beaches, all accessible by land.

# Serifos

**HISTORY:** Serifos was first mentioned in mythology as the place where the hero Perseus was washed ashore with his mother Danae and then set off to subdue the fearsome Medusa. It was colonized by the Ionians around the 10th century, joined the Athenian Confederacy, and submitted to the Macedonians and Ptolemies. A place of exile for Roman political prisoners, Serifos experienced further decline under the Byzantines and was later governed by Venetian feudal lords. After being sacked by Barbarossa (1537), it fell into the hands of the Turks. For a short period (1770-1774) the island was occupied by the Russians. In recent years it has been very popular among tourists, even though it is equipped with few of the usual amenities.

**SIGHTSEEING:** The capital, with its ruined Venetian castle, dazzling white houses and flag stoned lanes, is one of the loveliest in the

*Area: 73 sq. km. **Population:** 1,133 **Capital:** Serifos or Hora*
*How to get there: By daily boat from Piraeus,*
*Sifnos, Kimolos, Milos*

Cyclades. A small collection of archaeological finds from the island is housed in the Town Hall. A number of post-Byzantine churches exist, most of them renovated. In the southwest part of the island, near Koutala, a cave used for cult worship has been discovered but has yet to be developed. The same area possesses two Hellenistic towers, called Aspropyrgos and Psaropyrgos today.

Churches and monasteries are scattered throughout the island. In the north, near the village of Panaya, lies the Byzantine church of the same name, an important construction of the 10th or 11th century. West of Panayia there is the church of Agios Stefanos, whose walls show traces of Byzantine frescoes. However, the village's most outstanding monument is the 17th century monastery of the Taxiarches near the village of Galani. This small fortress-like complex contains frescoes renovated in the 18th century along with sacred treasures, precious books and manuscripts.

Serifos is a stony, mountainous island with tiny valleys tucked in between the hills and peaks. Though one of the most barren places in Greece, it is well endowed with beautiful beaches with clear water, accessible either by caique or on foot. The easiest to reach are Livadi, Koutalas, Megalo Livadi, Psilli Ammos, Ramos and Sykamia. The island has yet to be developed for tourism. All the hotels and rooms for rent are located at Livadi, the port; only a few rooms are available in the Hora. Nevertheless, its considerable natural beauty attracts an ever-growing number of visitors.

# Kythnos

**HISTORY:** On Kythnos, in the region of Loutra, traces of a human settlement older than any other in the Cyclades, dating to 7500 BC, have been brought to light. During the Mycenaean era, the island was inhabited by the Dryopids. It saw the Macedonians, Ptolemies and Romans come and go, and centuries later belonged to the Duchy of Naxos. Governed by the Gozzadinis from 1337, it fell to the Turks in 1617.

**SIGHTSEEING:** Merichas, the island's harbour, lies on its west side. Near there, at Voriokastro, the ruins of an ancient city that flourished until the Roman era can be seen. To the north of the capital, in the interior of the island, there are the ruins of a Hellenistic tower. There are numerous post-Byzantine churches with finely carved icon screens and icons painted in the Cretan-Venetian style. To the southeast stands the Monastery of Panayia Kanala. Apart from

*Area:* 99 sq. km. *Population:* 1,502
*Capital:* Messaria or Hora
*How to get there:* By boat from Lavrion, Kea and Piraeus

the Hora and Merichas, Kythnos has two other villages – Dyropida, with its marvelous, but undeveloped Katafyki cave, and Loutra, known for its mineral waters. North of Loutra, at Palaiokastro, there are the ruins of the medieval capital and Venetian castle. The island has lovely beaches accessible by car or caique. In the northwest, the islet of Agios Loukas is linked to its larger neighbour by a narrow strip of sand.

# Sifnos

**HISTORY:** The island was initially inhabited by the Phoenicians and the Carians who called it Akys or Meropia. They were followed by the Minoans who changed its name to Minoa. From that time on it shared the fate of the rest of the Cyclades, flourishing particularly from the time it was colonized by the Ionians until the Classical era. As a member of the Athenian Confederacy it took part in the Persian Wars. The extent of Sifnos power and wealth, stemming from its gold and silver mines, is reflected in the magnificent treasure its citizens dedicated to Apollo at Delphi. Under the Byzantine empire it belonged to the Theme of the Aegean, passing in 1207 to the Venetians and the Duchy of Naxos. Though it was sacked by Barbarossa in 1537, its feudal rulers, the Gozzadinis, managed to hold onto the island until 1617 when it passed to the Turks. Sifnos was active in the

*Area:* 74 sq. km. **Population:** 2,027 **Capital:** Apollonia
***How to get there:*** By boat daily from Piraeus, Serifos, Kimolos, Milos and in summer regular local connections with Paros

struggle for independence, which it won at the same time as the rest of the Cyclades.

**SIGHTSEEING:** Finds from excavations at Agios Andreas, Kalamitsi and Agios Nikitas prove that the island was inhabited from the Prehistoric through Hellenistic age without any interruption. Near Platys Yialos there are ruins of a Hellenistic tower. The capital, Apollonia, is built like an amphitheatre on the

sides of three low hills in the heart of the island. Its old mansions and churches are particularly attractive, and there one can visit an exhibition of folk arts and crafts. Kastro, built on a precipitous rock on the east coast of the island, was inhabited in prehistoric times as digs of the British School of Archaeology reveal. Up to 1836 it was the capital of Sifnos. While ancient traces date from the 8th century BC, the castle itself belongs to the 14th century. The most impressive Byzantine monument on the island is the monastery of Prophitis Ilias, dating from the 8th century. Other monasteries worth visiting are Vrysi (16th c.), Chrysostomos (1550), and Panayia of Chrysopighi (17th c.). At Seralia one can detect the outlines of the mediaeval harbour installations.

Sifnos is graced with several villages of great charm (Artemonas, Agios Andreas, Katavati) and many superb beaches (Kamares, Chrysopighi, Hersoniso, etc.). Ideally suited for quiet holidays, it attracts rather sophisticated visitors and offers a wide choice of accommodation.

# Kimolos

**HISTORY:** A mountainous island, Kimolos is known for its fuller's earth, a stony material used in the manufacture of porcelain. According to the myth the hero Kimolos founded the first settlement on the island and gave it his name. Its history is linked from antiquity with that of Milos, on which it has always depended. During the Frankish occupation, it went by the name of Argentiera and was used as a hideout by pirates.

**SIGHTSEEING:** The ruins of ancient Kimolos lie in the area of Ellinika, 4 km. southwest of the capital. At Limni- Varvarakaina there is a cave with tombs, similar to the catacombs on Milos; other caves exist at Kako Potamo and Vromolimni. At Palaiokastro one can see the remains of a small tower known as Portara. The capital (1 km. North of the harbour, Psathi) is built around the mediaeval castle. The inner castle dates from the 13th or 14th century, the outer

*Area: 36 sq. km. Population: 786 Capital: Kimolos*
*How to get there: By boat from Piraeus, caiques to and*
*from neighbouring islands*

castle from the 17th. Of the older churches, Christos (1592) and Evangelistria (1608) are the most interesting. Two archaeological collections may be viewed, one at the museum, the other at the Afentakio Foundation.

The island is blessed with lovely beaches, easy to reach by caique or on foot, but it has yet to be developed for tourism. A fine place for a tranquil holiday.

# Milos

**HISTORY:** Inhabited since prehistoric times, Milos was one of the most advanced islands during the Cycladic era. In the second and first millennium, it was invaded in turn by the Cretans, the Mycenaeans and the Dorians. In 416 BC it was laid waste by the Athenians as punishment for its neutrality in the Peloponnesian War. But prosperity returned under the Macedonians and the Romans. Successively subjected to pirate raids, Venetian reconstruction and Turkish occupation, Milos was liberated in 1821.

**SIGHTSEEING:** Milos owes its mineral wealth to the volcano submerged in the depths of its harbour (Adama). Objects from Milos found at diverse ancient Greek sites testify to its high level of culture. The capital is typically Cycladic in style. Its archaeological museum contains artifacts from the Neolithic to the Modern era, while folk arts and crafts are housed in a 19th century building. The ancient city was discovered at Klima; in 1820 the famous statue of Aphrodite now in the Louvre was found there.

*Area: 151 sq. km. Population: 4,554 Capital: Milos or Plaka*
*How to get there: By boat from Piraeus*
*the other Cyclades, Crete and the Dodecanese*

Twenty years later excavations revealed the famous early Christian catacombs. Near the village of Apollonia lie traces of the prehistoric city of Phylakope. Milos also boasts a number of Byzantine churches and monasteries (Panayia ston Kipo, 5th c.). To the southwest of the island there are the caves, dubbed "the Meteora of the Sea", and the Emerald Grotto. To the north there are several rocky islets of volcanic origin, of which the most impressive is Glaronisia.

# Paros-Antiparos

**HISTORY:** Inhabited since prehistoric times, Paros flourished particularly during the early Cycladic era (3200-2100 BC), though it seems subsequently to have been deserted until the Mycenaean period. The island attracted Minoan, Arcadian, Achaean settlers and around 1000 BC Ionians. From the 8th century till the start of the Persian Wars, Paros experienced great prosperity thanks to its marble quarries. During the 6th and 5th centuries it was home to a school of sculpture and arts and letters were especially cultivated. Later, governed by Macedonians and Romans, Paros was insignificant during the Byzantine era and was occupied by the Venetians in 1207, falling to the Turks in the 16th century. From 1770 to 1774 it was the basis of the Russian fleet commanded by Orloff and took an active part in the fight for independence.

*Area:* 195 sq. km. **Population:** 7,830 **Capital:** Paros or Parikia
**How to get there:** By boat from Piraeus and Rafina, by air
from Athens, Crete, Rhodes, linked with the other Cyclades

**SIGHTSEEING:** The capital, occupying the site of the ancient city, lies on the west coast of the island. At its highest point, the former acropolis, there are the ruins of a castle constructed with material from the temple to Demeter.

Several Byzantine and post Byzantine churches are scattered unobtrusively throughout the town; the most important is the impressive 4th century Panayia Katapoliani.

Of the finds exhibited in the archaeological museum, the Parian Chronicle, a history of the island from the 16th century to 263 BC, stands out.

Ancient sanctuaries have been discovered at Dilion (to Apollo) and on Kounado hill (to Aphrodite and Eileithyia).

More Byzantine and post-Byzantine churches abound in the island's picturesque villages, while monasteries with valuable icons and wall paintings are scattered throughout the countryside (Thapsani and Agios Antonios monasteries, etc.). Naoussa with its whitewashed houses and modern tourist facilities is one of Paro's most charming districts. On the east coast, Marpissa with its Venetian castle and the area of Psytopiani are worth a visit.

Caiques to Antiparos, the largest of the neighbouring islands (area 35 sq. km., pop.

635), leave from Pounta on the west coast. Antiparos was first settled in the Neolithic era. The town is built around a Venetian castle. Its famous cave, richly ornamented with stalagmites, and the church of St. John the Cave Dweller are located on the west coast. Both islands are surrounded by marvelous beaches. Paros is fully equipped to serve tourists and combines quiet holidays with cosmopolitan surroundings.

# Folegandros

**HISTORY:** The first inhabitants mentioned are the Carians, followed by the Phoenicians and the Cretans. Folegandros was later colonized by the Dorians and the Ionians and later joined the Athenian Confederacy. Subjugated by the Romans, in 1207 it became part of the Duchy of Naxos and was governed by the Gozzodini family until 1607 when it fell to the Turks. The island was repeatedly devastated and raided by pirates.

**SIGHTSEEING:** The capital is built high above the port, Karavostasi, and consists of two parts. The older, more picturesque section lies in the area around the fortress (Kastro) erected by Marco Sanudo in 1212. This Kastro resembles the ones on Sifnos and Kimolos. At Palaiokastro one can see remains of the fortifications and houses of the ancient city.

Tucked into the walls is the Church of Panayia, the most beautiful on the island. The cave of

*Area:* 31 sq. km. *Population:* 567 *Capital:* Folegandros
*How to get there:* By boat from Piraeus, Crete,
the Dodecanese and other Cyclades

Chrysospilia with stalagmites and stalactites is still unexplored; in ancient times it appears to have been set aside for cult worship. Tiny settlements exist at Ano Meria, while at Kastelli there are ruins of a small fortress.

The beaches of Agios Georgios and Livadi offer good swimming. Lacking amenities and roads, the island has few rooms for rent. Visitors in search of quiet will find it here.

# Amorgos

**HISTORY:** Amorgos was first inhabited in prehistoric times. Its growth coincided with the peak of the Cycladic civilization. Figurines remarkable for the harmony of their proportions have been discovered on the island, which is also famous for "the Amorgos chiton" and a red dye produced for export up to the 17th century. In antiquity, three autonomous cities existed – Aighiali, Arkesini and Minoa, of which ruins and coins have been found. The island was colonized by the Ionians and the Samians and was a member of the Athenian Confederacy. In the Hellenistic era it was subdued by both the Ptolemies and the Romans, later suffering persistent pirate raids during the Byzantine period.

**SIGHTSEEING:** Apart from the ruins of the three ancient cities, a collection of archaeological finds is housed in an 18th century mansion in Hora. Ruins of Hellenistic towers can be seen near the villages of Richti, Terlaki, Katapola and Arkesini, and Byzantine monuments are scat-

*Area: 121 sq. km.* **Population:** *2,100* **Capital:** *Amorgos of Hora*
**How to get there:** *By boat from Piraeus and the other*
*Cyclades, and in summer from Rafina*

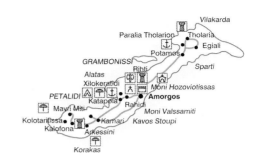

tered all over the island. The capital also boasts a 13th century Venetian castle. Worth visiting are the monasteries of Hozoviotissa (11th c.), perched on a rock 300 m. high, and of St. John the Theologian, as well as the churches of Panayia Katapoliani and Agios Nikolaos.

The island has not yet been fully developed for tourism but is ideal for a quiet holiday. The beaches near Katapola are easily reached by land or by sea, while the others entail a trip by caique.

# Syros

**HISTORY:** The history of the island begins with the Neolithic Age. Finds at Kastri and Halandriani belong to the early Cycladic period (2700-2000 BC). The first inhabitants were Phoenicians, followed in the 10th and 9th century by Ionian colonists who founded two cities, one where Ermoupolis now stands. Like the surrounding islands, it joined the Athenian Confederacy, and was ruled by successive waves of Macedonians, Ptolemies and Romans. Undergoing a decline during the Byzantine era, it too belonged to the Duchy of Naxos until 1537 when the Turks overthrew the Franks. Many Catholics took refuge to the island, and with the support of Venice and France it became a bastion of Catholicism. Syros enjoyed great prosperity in the years before and after the Revolution.

**SIGHTSEEING:** The capital, built in 1822, impresses the visitor with its old mansions and distinctive local architecture. The Public Theatre is a copy in miniature of Milan's La Scala. There are several noteworthy finds exhibited in the museum. Ano Syros, the capital under the Franks,

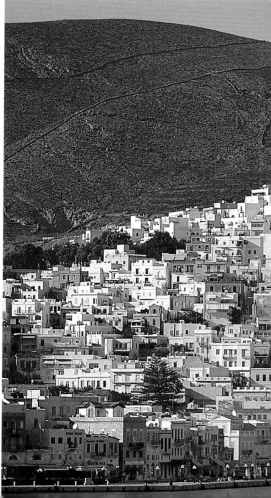

*Area:* 84 sq. km. *Population:* 19,668 *Capital:* Ermoupolis
*How to get there:* By boat from Piraeus and Rafina, linked
with the other Cyclades, Crete, Ikaria, Samos and Fourni.

has kept its mediaeval character virtually intact. At Halandriani, a prehistoric cemetery was discovered, while at Kastri there are remains of a fortified settlement, among the oldest in the Cyclades.

Medieval monuments and Byzantine churches abound in Syros, e.g. the Capuchin and Jesuit monastery, the church of Agios Georgios, and the Faneromeni monastery. But there are also quaint villages and glorious beaches well worth exploring such as at Vari, Poseidonia, Galissa, etc.

# Naxos

**HISTORY:** The first inhabitants on Naxos were Thracians who brought with them the worship of Dionysus. They were followed by Carians and Ionians. Naxos began to prosper during the Mycenaean era and reached its peak in the 7th and 6th centuries BC. Dominated in quick succession by the Macedonians, the Ptolemies, the Egyptians, the Rhodians and the Romans, it suffered constant pirate raids under the Byzantines. In 1207, Marco Sanudo captured the island and made it the seat of his dukedom (the Duchy of Naxos or the Archipelago). Laid waste by Barbarossa in 1537, it belonged to Iosiph Naxis from 1566 to 1579 and thereafter was occupied by the Turks. Naxos was liberated with the rest of the Cyclades.

**SIGHTSEEING:** Naxos has inherited many monuments from the different eras of its rich history. On the west coast lies the capital, dominated by its Venetian castle. Built in 1207 by Marco Sanudo, it was populated largely by Catholics. Inside the castle walls there are the Ursuline

*Area:* 428 sq. km. **Population:** 16,703 **Capital:** Naxos
*How to get there:* By boat from Piraeus and Rafina,
links with the other Cyclades and Crete

and Capuchin monasteries as well as the old school of commerce, now the archaeological museum. The Byzantine and Folk Museum is housed in a restored tower. The castle also contains the Catholic cathedral, and Byzantine and post-Byzantine churches are scattered all over the town. One can still see the huge doorway of the 6th century temple of Apollo standing free on the islet at the entrance to the harbour. Excavations at Grotta and Aplomata have unearthed early Cycladic and Geometric

finds proving that Naxos was one of the centres of the Cycladic civilization. In Agidia there are remains of an ancient temple. One of the most beautiful areas in Naxos is Tragaia in the interior. There are several Venetian towers on the island (Halki, Potamia, Polochni), while Moni claims the oldest Byzantine church of Our Lady Drosiani (6th c.).

Near Filoti there is a hill called Za with a cave dedicated to the cult worship of Bacchus (local tradition maintains that it was the birthplace of Zeus). At Apeiratho, which has a strong Venetian atmosphere, there are several towers with names like Sommaripa, Crispi and Sforza. The museum there contains interesting early Cycladic finds. There are more towers – Della Rocca, Palaiologos and Barozzi by name – at Sagri and further south the ruined medieval castle of Apalyros. Apollonia is famous for its colossal kouros of the god Apollo (7th c. BC).

Naxos offers superb beaches on the west side of the island, which has a good road network and tourist accommodations. It has much to offer the visitor who loves to explore.

# The Smaller Cyclades

**A. THE SMALLER CYCLADES:** These are the ten tiny islands lying between Ios and Amorgos. They are connected by ferryboat twice a week with Piraeus via Amorgos. Isolated, lacking amenities, but blessed with unspoiled natural environment and crystal-clear seas, they are ideal for vacationers seeking a return to nature. Most of them have been inhabited since prehistoric times and share a common history, confirmed by the presence of ancient and medieval ruins. The most important finds of the prehistoric era were discovered at Keros.

**B. SIKINOS** *(area: 41 sq. km., pop.: 290):* Inhabited since the Mycenaean era, it shared the fate of the other Cyclades. It was governed by the Dacotini and Gozzadini families from 1207 till the 17th century, when the Turks captured it. It was liberated in 1821. Virtually nothing remains of the old capital at Kastro, but there are ruins of the ancient city at Agia Marina and of a Herron at Episkopi.

# Sikinos-Anafi

**C. ANAFI** *(area: 38 sq. km., pop.: 471):* First settled by the Phoenicians, it followed the course
of its neighbours. At Kastelli and Katalimatsa
there are some ruined houses. To the south
near the ancient sanctuary of Apollo the Monastery of Our Lady Kalamiotissa stood, of
which only the church remains.

None of these islands have been developed
for tourism, but what they lack in amenities,
they more than make up for in untouched
charm and unpolluted seas.

# Ios

**HISTORY:** Some legends link Ios with the birth and death of Homer. First inhabited by the Phoenicians, the island was later colonized by the Ionians around the 10th century. Ios belonged to the Athenian Confederacy and was subsequently ruled by the Ptolemies of Egypt. During the Roman era it was designated as a place of exile. After the collapse of Byzantium, it fell to the Venetians, being a part of the Duchy of Naxos. The Turks took over the island in 1537. For centuries a prey to pirate raids, it was also used as a pirate lair at times. Ios took an active part in the War of Independence.

**SIGHTSEEING:** The capital, built atop the ancient city, is some distance above the harbour (Ormos). A 14th century Venetian castle looks down on the town from the heights of the ancient acropolis. The town with its little

*Area:* 108 sq. km. *Population:* 1,451 *Capital:* Ios or Hora
*How to get there:* By boat from Piraeus, Crete
and the other Cyclades

white houses and steep flag stoned alley-ways is permeated with the characteristic Cycladic charm. Three churches stand out: the Prodromos, Agioi Anargyroi, and, on the site formerly occupied by a temple of Apollo, St. Catherine's.

On the north side of the town stand some stately windmills -a typical sight in the Cyclades. Overlooking the bay of Agia Theodoti on the east coast of the island there is the

shell of a medieval castle. A bit higher up, near the village of Psathi, there are traces of antiquities. Plakoto, on the north coast of the island, boasts "Homer's tomb" and the remains of a Hellenistic tower. Especially noteworthy is the plethora of title churches, scattered all over the island, which are said to number over 300.

The shores of Ios are indented with numerous picturesque coves lapped by crystal-clear water. They can be reached either by car or caique, and many are within walking distance from Hora (Kalamos, Psathi, Manganari, Agia Theodoti). Mylopota, with its wonderful sand (served by local bus), attracts crowds of tourists.

Ios is well equipped to accommodate visitors in both hotels and rooms, while development and improvement are ongoing to meet the ever-increasing popularity of this delightful island.

# Mykonos

**HISTORY:** Mykonos today is one of the best-known and most cosmopolitan islands in Greece. Its fame overshadows that of the other Cyclades. In antiquity, however, the exact opposite was true. Very little is known about the island's history, and in all likelihood it played an insignificant role. Though Mykonos was colonized by the Ionians in the 10th or the 9th century, its poor contribution to the Athenian Confederacy indicates that it was neither rich nor powerful. The island had two cities in ancient times, one on the west coast near the present capital, the other in the north near Palaiokastro. Under the Ptolemies and the Romans it prospered to some degree, only to sink into obscurity once more during the Byzantine era. From 1207 to 1390, together with Tinos, it belonged to the Ghizi family and was subsequently a Venetian province. Sacked by Barbarossa (1537) and subjugated by the

*Area:* 85 sq. km. *Population:* 5,530 *Capital:* Mykonos
*How to get there:* By air from Athens, Crete, Rhodes, Santorini;
by boat from Piraeus, Rafina and the other Cyclades

Turks, its inhabitants soon turned to piracy for a livelihood. An important event in local history was the formation of the Commune of Mykoniates in 1615. From the 18th century on, the island began to flourish. It developed a distinguished merchant fleet and enjoyed economic prosperity. Mykonos was the birthplace of the Revolutionary hero, Manto Mavroyenous. Since the 50s, tourism has brought the island unprecedented wealth.

**SIGHTSEEING:** The capital lies on the west side of the island, beneath the scant remains of a Venetian fortress (Kastro). This old neighbourhood claims the town's pre-eminent landmark, the Church of Virgin Paraportiani, the most important of the island's 400 churches. Its unique architecture combines Byzantine, vernacular and Western features. The south part of town, with its picturesque houses and wooden balconies, is the famous "Venice of Myconos" or Alevkantra. The main square is dominated by the Cathedral and an old Catholic church. The island's trademark, the charming windmills, stand a bit further

away apparently on the site of the ancient city. The archaeological museum contains finds from nearby Renia. Worth visiting are also the Municipal Library, the Folk Museum and the recently opened Naval Museum.

At Lino there is a ruined tower, while an underground cistern, known as Yiannaros well, has been found near Platys Yialos. Ano Mera is the site of the monastery of Virgin Tourliani, built in 1541 and restored in 1767. It is known for the sculpted decoration on its bell tower and for its Western stylistic elements. Palaiokastro has given its name to a 17th century monastery; ruins of the old fortress can still be seen. Finds from the Archaic and Classical periods indicate that the hill behind the monastery was inhabited in antiquity, while at Panormou Bay and Mavri Spilia prehistoric remains and a vast quantity of geometric artifacts have been discovered.

There is a beach on Mykonos for every taste. Among the most beautiful are Kalafatis, Platys Yialos, Elia, Agia Anna, Orno, with Paradise and Super Paradise reserved for nudists.

The island is amply endowed with the full range of tourist accommodation and amenities, but at the peak of the season even its numerous hotels and rooms cannot begin to house the hordes of tourists attracted by its unique charm.

# Delos

Delos *(area: 3.5 sq. km.)*, the sacred island of antiquity, is uninhabited today. Several boats a day ferry visitors from nearby Mykonos.

It was here that, according to myth, Leto repaired to give birth to Artemis and Apollo. Inhabited as early as 3000 BC, it was originally called Ortygia. In the 9th century BC it became the headquarters of an Ionian league. The Ionians had colonized all the Aegean islands and later, in the 6th century, the Atheni-ans took advantage of their kinship with the Ionians to infiltrate the league. In 540 BC the first purification, i.e. the removal of tombs from the sacred area, took place. In 478 BC it became the centre of the Athenian (or Delian) Confederacy and in 426 a second purification was carried out. At this time, the bones of the dead were transferred to Renia (a neighbouring islet), and from then on no births or deaths were permitted on Delos.

During the Hellenistic era, Delos was able to free itself of Athenian influence. Mithradates ransacked the island in 88 BC, destroying monuments in his wake, while only 19 years later Delos was sacked again – a catastrophe from which it never recovered – and remained deserted. The ruins were discovered by foreign travellers in the 15th century. Since 1871 the French School of Archaeology has been responsible for the excavations.

The island is an archaeological site in itself. Beginning with the west coast and the sacred harbour, moving northwest, one comes to the Propylaia and the Agora of the Competialists (2nd c.), followed by the Sacred Way with the statue bases. To the west lies the Stoa of Philip (3rd c.) with the Agora of the Delians opposite. The foundations of the Temple of Apollo, the Oikos and Stoa of the Naxians and, to the north, the Keraton and the Temple of Artemis (2nd c.) can still be seen, as can the Prytaneion (5th c.), the Temple of Dionysus, the Ekklesias-

terion, the Agora of the Italians and the Temple of Leto. Near the temple lies the famous Terrace of the Lions, dedicated by the Naxians in the 7th century. Five of the original nine lions have been preserved. In the quarter near the Theatre, the floors of the houses, Hellenistic and Roman, were decorated with mosaics. Finds from the site are housed in the museum on the island, near which 17 of the original 26 rows of seats of the Theatre have preserved. There is so much to see on Delos that a full list in a guide this size is impossible.

# Tinos

**HISTORY:** In ancient times, the island was called Ophiousa. It has been settled since the Bronze Age. Famed for its marble and stonework, Tinos flourished particularly during the 3rd and 2nd century BC. After its conquest by the Romans, it sank into obscurity. With the fall of Constantinople to the Franks, it passed into Venetian hands until it was occupied by the Turks in 1715. In 1822 a miraculous icon of the Virgin was found on the island, making it ever since the destination of thousands of pilgrims every year. In 1940 the Italians sank the Greek warship Helle in Tinos harbour.

**SIGHTSEEING:** The capital was founded after 1715. Its most striking landmark is the Church of the Virgin built in 1823 to house the icon. There are two museums, one showing the work of Tinian and other modern Greek artists, the other exhibiting archaeological finds. The Monastery of Agia Triada (1610) contains a collection of folk arts and crafts. The countryside and villages are full of

*Area: 194 sq. km. **Population:** 7,730 **Capital:** Tinos*
*How to get there: By boat from Piraeus, Rafina*
*and the other Cyclades*

the richly decorated dovecotes for which
the island is famous.

Remains of the Venetian castle and the mediaeval city may be seen at Steni, while near
Kardiani there are the ruins of a Hellenistic
tower. The church of Agios Athanasios (1453),
one of the oldest on Tinos, and the monastery
of Panayia Katapoliani (1786) are in the vicinity of Ysternia. Tinos possesses its own beauty,
with its small villages sprinkled through its
verdant landscape, but it has little in the way
of tourist amenities.

# Andros

**HISTORY:** Little is known of the island's ancient history. It was colonized by the Ionians at the start of the historical era and came into close contact with Athens and Euboea. Andros enjoyed particular prosperity from the 7th to 4th century BC. Though it was allied with the Persians in 480 BC, it later joined the Athenian Confederacy. Subjugated by the Macedonians during the Hellenistic era, it was later captured by the Romans who ceded it to Attalos of Pergamon. In Byzantine times it was a centre for silk production and suffered constant pirate raids. Becoming part of the Duchy of Naxos in 1207, it was governed by Marino Dandolo. The Turks occupied the island in 1566, and in 1821 its population rose in rebellion led by Theofilos Kairis.

**SIGHTSEEING:** The capital, in the same location as the mediaeval town, is situated on the southeast side of the island. A ruined Venetian

*Area: 380 sq. km. Population: 9,020 Capital: Andros*
*How to get there: By boat from Rafina, Tinos,*
*Mykonos, Paros and Naxos*

castle and an arched bridge spanning the old
moat still survive. The town boasts an archae-
ological-naval museum and a museum of
modern art. Its most noteworthy churches are
Panayia Palatiani and Panayia Hodigitria.

To the south, near the lovely village of Men-
ites, lie the ruins of mediaeval towers and of
the church of the Madonna of Koumoulos.
Messaria was the capital of the island in the
18th and 19th centuries; here, one can see the

ancestral tower of the Kairis family and the church of the Taxiarches built by the emperor Manuel Komninos (1143-1180), which contains a fine 18th century marble icon screen. At Fallika, the monastery of Panachrantos was founded in 961 by Nikephoros Phokas. The famous Sariza mineral water of Andros gushes from springs at Apikia, where there is also an 18th century monastery (Agios Nikolaos).

The scenery between Korthi and Andros makes the area one of the most beautiful on the island; it is dotted with picturesque villages and mediaeval towers (Kochylos, Aprovato). At Zagora, finds dating from the Geometric period (8th c. BC) have been excavated, while the ancient city and the acropolis lie below the modern village of Palaiopolis. The northern part of Andros, much more sparsely settled, has some ruined Venetian towers (Makrotanalo, Varidi) and the monastery of Zoodochos Pighi, protector of the island.

There are beaches all around the island; some of the better known are at Nimborio, Paraporti, Batsi, etc. Andros offers many hotels and rooms, particularly in the vicinity of Batsi and the capital.

# Santorini (Thira)

**HISTORY:** Santorini's wild beauty and volcanic landscape distinguish it from the rest of the Cyclades. Its present shape is what remained after the sinking of the Kaldera (Crater) of the (now extinct) volcano, which is encircled by the islets of Thirasia and Aspronisi. In antiquity it was called Strongyli (round) or Kallisti (most beautiful) and was first settled by the Phoenicians. Inhabited since prehistoric times, it flourished during the early Cycladic period and afterwards, as shown by the excavations at Akrotiri. All its prosperity came to an end, however, with the eruption of the volcano around 1600 BC. At the start of the first millennium Dorian colonists settled there and the island took a new name, Thera, after their leader. Subsequently, special contacts were developed with Cyprus, Crete, Asia Minor and several regions on the Greek mainland. Allied with Sparta until 426 BC

*Area: 76 sq. km. **Population:** 7,083 **Capital:** Fira*
*How to get there: By air from Athens, Crete, Rhodes and*
*Mykonos; by boat from Piraeus and other Aegean islands*

when the island joined the Athenian Confederacy, it was used as a refuge from the Ptolemies because of its location, falling into decline during the Roman era. Its strategic location was again of importance during the
Byzantine Empire. From 1207 it belonged to
the Dukes of Naxos and was governed by a
series of Venetian lords (Barozzi, Crispo, Pisa-
ni). Despite its good fortifications, it still suffered frequent pirate raids. It was ceded to

Iosiph Naxis and in 1579 fell to the Turks. In 1821 it took an active part in the Revolution and shipping brought considerable prosperity to it in the later 19th century. The long Latin occupation left its mark on the island, and Western influence can also be seen in the large numbers of Catholics among the population.

**SIGHTSEEING:** Fira, the island's capital, it built along the upper slopes of the west coast. It is linked to the harbour by a steep, stepped road and by cable car, from which one has a superb view over the harbour and shoreline. Its houses are built in a style unique to the island. Small, dazzlingly white, with numerous windows and vaulted roofs they present a stunning picture, in which the larger mansions and the Archaeological Museum stand out. At the Dominican monastery there is a weaving school and cultural centre. The Catholic cathedral is located near the monastery, while the Orthodox cathedral is in the southern part of the town. The aristocratic

families used to live at Imerovigli where there are ruins of old mansions and the monastery of Agios Nikolaos (1674).

Skaros is the site of one of the island's most important fortresses. Abandoned in the 17th century, this was the mediaeval capital. From Fira Bay ,one can take trips to the volcano, Nea Kammeni and Old Kammeni, where there are hot springs.

Akrotiri in the southern tip of the island was the site of the prehistoric city of Thera. Excavations have brought to light an entire city

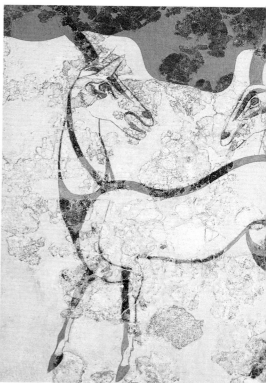

with houses, streets, squares and workshops that collapsed when the volcano erupted. At the village named La Ponte by the Venetians there are the ruins of another fortified castle, with two churches. Mesa Vouno, on the other hand, is the site of ancient Thera. Here one can see the ruins of the agora, theatre, public and private buildings, but of the finds an Archaic clay idol, completely intact, is the most impressive. The village of Vothonas is very picturesque with its churches of the Virgin stin Trypa and Agia Anna, as is Pyrgos with its Byzantine church Theotakaki (10th c.). At Mesa Gonia, another Byzantine church, the 11th century Episkopi, containing valuable icons and distinctive frescoes has been preserved. The monastery of Prophitis Elias (18th c.) has a collection of holy treasures and also op-

erates a folk museum and icon-painting studio. At Megalohori there are the ruins of a little 3rd century BC temple. Ia and Finikia on the north ridge of the island are two of Santorini's most attractive settlements, their whitewashed houses a brilliant contrast to the vividly painted vaulted roofs.

Most of the beaches on Santorini have black sand and pumice pebbles, a result of their volcanic origin. Kamari and Perissa are among the best. Though the south coast lends itself better to swimming and water sports, there are beaches in the north at Ia, Ammoudi and Armeni. Small boats leave Ia for excursions to the islet of Thirasia opposite.

Santorini's unusual landscape, its distinctive architecture, the wealth and diversity of its monuments attract floods of visitors particularly in summer. As a result accommodation is hard to come by at this time, despite the ample number of rooms and hotels. For all its popularity, Santorini's beauty and charm have not been affected. The island offers both cosmopolitan pleasures and simple delights in its far-flung villages. Hotels to satisfy all tastes abound and taking a room in a private house will acquaint the visitor with the islander's unforgettable hospitality.

# Euboea

**HISTORY:** The second largest island in Greece, Euboea has been inhabited since the Neolithic era. During the Mycenaean age, it developed trade links with the Cyclades. By the 8th century BC two of its cities, Chalkis and Eretria, had become prosperous and powerful enough to found colonies in southern Italy. In later years, it fell under the domination of Athens, Macedonia and Rome (194 BC). For centuries a Byzantine province, it submitted to the Franks in 1204 and became a Venetian posses-sion in 1366 under the name of Negreponte. Euboea was occupied by the Turks from 1470 until its liberation in 1829.

**SIGHTSEEING:** The capital, Chalkis (88 km from Athens), is a modern town, built on the narrow Euripus channel whose famous rip tides separate the island from the mainland. The city has an incredibly long history, having been settled in Neolithic times and reaching its peak in the 8th century BC. Few reminders

*Area:* 3,654 sq. km. **Population:** 185,626 **Capital:** Chalkis
**How to get there:** By car and ferryboat from Oropos,
Rafina, Arkitsa, Volos and the Sporades

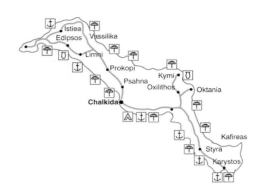

of this ancient city that lay somewhere to the east of the present town have survived. Remains of the medieval and Turkish fortress may be seen on the hill opposite. Chalkis has a Fine Arts Museum. From Chalkis roads lead both to mountain villages with Byzantine churches and picturesque fountains surrounded by lush vegetation (Katheni, Steni, Dirfys, etc.) and to southern Euboea. At southern Euboea, one can enjoy the attractively developed beach of Malakontas; Eretria, whose

8th century BC archaeological site lies near a popular resort area; Aliveri (ancient Tamynai), to wind up at Kymi, the biggest town on the east coast of the island, near the hot springs of Honeftikos.

In the southern part of the island, which possesses considerable facilities for tourists, it is worth visiting Dystos (the ancient city of the Dryopes), Styra and Karystos, which has a direct ferry link with Rafina. Monuments of both ancient and medieval times exist in Karystos, whose town plan was designed in 1841 by the Bavarian architect, Bierbach.

In Northern Euboea, which has experienced less tourist development, there are numerous charming, wooded hamlets offering opportunities for rest and relaxation. One of the most picturesque is Limni (occupying the site of ancient Elymnios), Pefki and Rovies. Aidipsos has been famous since antiquity for its therapeutic springs. The largest town in the area is Istiaia with its port Orei, which have been experiencing rapid growth in recent years.

Because of its proximity to Athens, Euboea is becoming increasingly popular; its peaceful villages and splendid beaches make it a wonderful choice for a holiday.

# SPORADES

To the southeast of the Prefecture of Magnisia (one of Thessaly's administrative divisions) and to the northeast of Evia (part of Mainland Greece) lies a chain of small islands by the name of the Sporades. The word in Greek refers to the concept of 'scattered', 'spread out at irregular intervals'. In the past all islands in the Aegean went by the name Sporades since they were scattered in geographical terms across the sea, compared to the Cyclades which formed a circle around the sacred island of Delos (Cyclades comes from the Greek word for circle which is the root of English words such as cycle and cyclical). Thus, there were Northern, Southern and Western Sporades. Today when we talk of the Northern Sporades or simply the Sporades we mean four large islands, Skiathos, Skopelos, Alonnisos and Skyros and numerous smaller islands in the surrounding maritime area. In administrative terms Skiathos, Skopelos and Alonnisos belong to the Prefecture of Magnisia while Skyros, lying further south, belongs to the Prefecture of Evia.

According to myth, three of the Sporades islands were created due to the struggle between the Titans Otos and Ephialtes. These two titans cast enormous rocks at each other, three of which fell into the sea forming Skiathos, Skopelos and Alonnisos.

The history of these islands was determined in large part by their fine position in the middle of the Aegean, in a key location for communication between southern and northern regions. For this reason, moreover, they were inhabited from early on. Archaeological excavations have brought to light traces of inhabitation from

the mid Paleolithic Age on Alonnisos (on the islet of Kokkinonisi or Vrachos to be precise) while settlements from the Neolithic Ages and Bronze Age have been found on the other islands. Finds show that the Sporades had developed commercial contacts with Limnos in the Eastern Aegean from the first phase of the Bronze Age. A significant settlement from the Mycenean Period existed on Skopelos, attested to by the domed tomb found in the area of Stafylos.

The area was settled in the 11th Century BC by Greeks, bringing about major social changes while later in the 8th century BC colonies were formed by refugees from Evia. During the classical period the islands took part in the Persian Wars and later joined the Athenian League and followed Athens' policy. During the Roman era they were raided by Sulla in the course of the First Mithridatic War (1st Century BC).

Under the Byzantines they fell into a state of decline and were used as a place of exile and were frequently attacked by pirates. From 1204 to 1538, with the exception of a few brief periods, they were under the control of the Franks Andre and Jeremiah Gizi. They were then seized by the Turks and were a battlefield between the Venetians and Turks. In the 1821 Revolution they contributed significantly to the struggle of the Greeks against the Turks and were finally liberated in 1830.

Today the Sporades attract a large number of foreign visitors having made massive leaps in development over recent years. Moreover, they are one of the main holiday destinations of residents of Central and Northern Greece due to their proximity to Volos. One of the main reasons for the increase in tourist influxes into the area is the outstanding natural beauty of the islands. In contrast to the most southerly islands of the Aegean, the Sporades are literally swathed in green with pine forests that reach right down to the shore. The sun-drenched beaches interspersed with wild, rocky stretches of

coastline, the clear waters and the picture postcard, traditional villages have something to satisfy even the most demanding visitor.

Skiathos, home to the major Greek writer, Alexandros Papadiamantis, is famed for its golden sandy beaches. It is the island visited by most holidaymakers compared to the other Sporades, giving it a somewhat cosmopolitan air. Skopelos, pine-covered from end to end, stands out for its picture postcard views and is ideal for carefree strolls along its traditional inland paths. An ideal place for relaxed holidays for from the bustling crowds of tourists is Skyros, the largest island in the chain where one can admire the characteristic, folk architecture. Alonnisos, with its emerald waters, is surrounded by a series of uninhabited smaller islands (Ayios Georgios, Yura, Dasia, Kyra Panayia, Xero, Peristera, Skantzoura and others) which demarcate the boundaries of the famed Alonnisos Marine Park. This park is a refuge for many rare, wild animal species, topped by the mediterranean seal (Monachus monachus). Caiques set off from Alonnisos bringing visitors to quite a few of these islets. It is not unusual for visitors to come across a group of dolphins diving around them playfully and following them until they return to land.

# Skiathos

**HISTORY:** The island's strategic location determined its fate in ancient times. The first settlers were Ionians, followed by colonists from neighbouring Chalkis. In 477 BC it joined the Athenian (or Delian) Confederacy. After short periods ruled by the Macedonians and the Romans, it eventually returned to Athenian hands. Like Skopelos, it belonged to the Ghizis (1207-1454) and was sacked by Barbarossa in 1538, surrendering to the Turks the following year. Its ships played an active role in the struggle for liberation, winning freedom in 1823. Skiathos is the birthplace of two famous modern Greek novelists: the "Saint" of modern Greek literature, Alexandros Papadiamantis (1851), and Alexandros Moraitidis.

**SIGHTSEEING:** Skiathos, the capital, presents a colourful, picturesque image with its tiled roofs, dazzling white houses and flower-filled court-

*Area:* 48 sq. km. *Population:* 4,127 *Capital:* Skiathos
*How to get there:* By air from Athens, or ferryboat from Agios
Konstantinos, Volos and Kymi; links with the other Sporades

yards. One of its most delightful spots is Bourtzi, the islet-site of a fortress constructed by the
Ghizis in 1270. On the west side the church of
Our Lady of Limnia rises. The house of Papadiamantis near the harbour now functions as a
museum. There are also a number of "arsenals"
where boats and caiques are made. Though
the present capital occupies the same location
as the ancient city, the fortified mediaeval capital, Kastro, lies to the north of the island. Here

dwelt the inhabitants until 1829, well out of the way of Turks and pirates; nowadays, nothing but ruins remain. Of the 30 old churches in Kastro, only three are preserved, among which the old Cathedral and the church of Christ. Several monasteries are scattered throughout the island, almost all possessing fine carved icon screens, wonderful frescoes and valuable icons. The monasteries of Evangelistria, Agios Haralambos and Our Lady of Kechria date from the 18th century. The monastery of Our Lady of Kounistra, which shelters a miracle-working icon, was built in 1727.

The island is noted for its greenery, its trees extending right to its golden beaches. One of the most splendid beaches in Greece is Lalaria with its Blue Grotto, where the sun creates fascinating reflections in the bluest of waters. Not to forget Koukounaries, renowned for its unsurpassed scenery. Or the beaches of Bourtzi, Plakes, Megas Yialos and the nudist beaches of Troulo and Banana.

Despite the crowds of tourists that descend on the island each summer, Skiathos manages to preserve its charm, along with tranquil corners where one can "get away from it all".

# Skopelos

**HISTORY:** Inhabited since the Mycenaean era (1600-1100 BC), Skopelos – the ancient Peparethos – became a colony of Chalkis (700 BC), passing to the Macedonians in 340 BC. Under the Byzantines it was a place of exile, while later it was taken over by the Venetian Ghizi family and joined to the Duchy of Naxos. Subsequently occupied by the Turks, it was freed during the War of Independence in 1821. It acquired its present name during the Hellenistic period.

**SIGHTSEEING:** The capital, one of the most picturesque of all island towns, is built on the slopes of a hill right on the sea. At its highest point lies the Kastro district with its remains of the Venetian castle erected by the Ghizis (13th c.). Here lived the modern Greek writer Pavlos Nirvanas whose house has been made into a museum. There are also here a ceramics workshop and the island's famous ovens where plums are dried into prunes. Of the many lovely churches, most noteworthy are

*Area:* 96 sq. km. ***Population:*** 4,451 ***Capital:*** Skopelos
***How to get there:*** By ferryboat from Agios Konstantinos,
Volos and Kymi; links with the other Sporades

those of Panayitsa, Agios Nikolaos and Evangelistria (17th and 18th c.).

The island is dotted with chapels and monasteries, the most important being the monasteries of Evangelistria (18th c.), Agia Varvara (1648) and Metamorphosis (1600). The beautiful beaches of Stafylos, Agnonta, Panormos and Velani can the reached either by car or caique. Generally speaking, Skopelos is a delightful, wooded island offering both quiet pleasures and sophisticated attractions.

# Alonissos

**HISTORY:** Alonissos has been inhabited since prehistoric times and was known to the ancients as Ikos or Liadromia. The subject of a conflict between the Macedonians and the Athenians, it shared the fate of the other islands and was continually raided by pirates before falling under Turkish domination. It suffered enormous damage during the 1965 earthquake, at which time the old hilltop capital was abandoned.

**SIGHTSEEING:** One can visit the ruins of the ancient city on the southeast side of the island at Kokkinokastro, where there are also the remains of a mediaeval castle. However, Alonnisos is primarily a spot for quiet holidays. The hotels are few though good, there are rooms for rent in private houses, but the road network is practically nonexistent. It is far easier to take a caique to the coastal villages and tranquil beaches around the is-

*Area:* 64 sq. km. *Population:* 1,528 *Capital:* Patitiri
*How to get there:* By ferryboat from Agios Konstantinos, Volos and Kymi; links with the other Sporades

land. In addition to Patitiri, the tiny capital, Alonnisos boasts two other villages: Palia (Old) Alonnisos (the former capital) and Votsi. Lovely beaches are found at Marpounta, Steni Vala and Kokkinokastro, where there are also traces of a Middle Palaeolithic settlement (100,000-33,000 BC). Surrounding the island are numerous uninhabited islets with exquisite beaches for swimming or fishing, all accessible by caique.

# Skyros

**HISTORY:** Since Homer's age Skyros has been known as the place where the legendary Achilles hid to escape going to Troy. Inhabited as early as the Neolithic era (5000 BC), it was later dominated by the Athenians who subsequently handed it over to the Romans. After the fall of Byzantium to the Franks, it was a Venetian possession until the Turkish Conquest. Skyros was liberated in 1829.

**SIGHTSEEING:** Skyros is very unusual from the geological point of view. A narrow isthmus sep-arates the northern, fertile and densely populated section from the southern, rocky and virtually inaccessible portion. Its charming capital, 11 km. from the port of Linaria, has two museums: one archaeological and folkloric, the other exhibiting both contemporary and older examples of traditional Skyrian arts and crafts (housed in the Faltaits mansion). Northeast of Hora lies the Castle, where there are ruins of the island's ancient acropolis (5th c. BC) as well as Byzantine and Venetian remains. Two churches stand apart from the rest – St. George's (936) in

*Area: 209 sq. km. **Population:** 2,757 **Capital:** Skyros (Hora)*
***How to get there:*** *By air from Athens or ferryboat*
*from Kymi and the other Sporades*

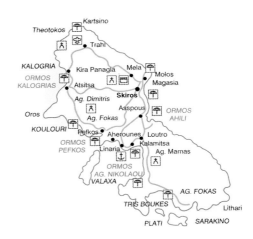

the monastery of the same name and Archontopanayia. A number of pottery workshops are located on the shore. One of Skyro's most famous landmarks is the memorial to the poet Rupert Brooke buried there in 1915.

Skyros' famous diminutive ponies live in the southern part of the island. The beaches of Pefkos, Acherounes, Treis Boukes, etc. can be reached by car.

Skyros is renowned for its rich folkloric tradition and distinctive architecture, as well as the diversity of its landscape.

# THE ISLANDS OF THE
# EASTERN AEGEAN

Cut off from the rest of the archipelago, the islands of the Eastern Aegean, together with the Dodecanese, are those closest to the shores of Asia Minor. Due to their position from time to time they have played a special role in Greek history. Hios and Samos are so close to Turkey's shores that one can simply go across with an ordinary boat in a matter of minutes. In addition to the two islands mentioned, this Eastern Aegean chain of islands also includes Lesbos (Mytilene), Ikaria, Fourni, Inousses and Psara.

All these islands were inhabited from early on. On Lesbos and Samos the first traces of inhabitation date back to the 4th millennium BC. The 3rd millennium BC was a period of major development with important settlements at Thermi on Lesbos and Emborio on Hios. During the entire Bronze Age close relations were built up with Asia Minor, the Cycladic islands and mainland Greece. Nonetheless, during the time of Minoan domination of the seas, after 1900 BC, commercial activities on the islands fell into decline and coastal settlements were abandoned. In the 12th century BC there were major upheavals in the Eastern Aegean and population shifts as the first Greek tribes moved onto the islands.

In the 10th century BC during the first wave of colonization the islands of the Eastern Aegean and the coast of Asia Minor opposite were inhabited by Ionians from Attica and around 800 BC 12 colonies from the area united to established the so-called Pan-Ionian League. In classical antiquity the islands flourished. Thanks to their geographical location they were exposed to innovations in intellectual and cultural areas, introducing new ideas from the nearly Orient.

During the 7th and 6th centuries BC Lesbos produced leading figures such as the poets Alcaeus, Terpandrus, Arion and Sappho, creators of lyric poetry and Pittacus, one of the seven sages of the ancient world. At that time too the major philosopher and mathematician Pythagoras was born there. Hios is considered to be the birthplace of Homer, the place were the great poet wrote the Iliad and the Odyssey. On Samos, during the reign of the tyrant Polycrates (6th century BC) progress was made in the fields of sculpture and architecture with glorious public works being built.

A turning point in the history of the islands was the Ionian Revolution (499 BC) which resulted in the islands being subjugated to the Persians from whom they were liberated after the end of the Persian Wars in 479 BC. Following this, the islands joined the Athenian League but broke away on several occasions and were punished by Athens with banishment, confiscation of property and the settlement of Athenians on their

of these flourished while others such as Ikaria were used for banishment. Of course, the pirate attacks which were rife at that time had a significant impact on their development. In 1204 with the fall of Constantinople to the Franks, the islands were integrated into the Latin Empire of Constantinople and in 1261 was granted to wealthy families from Venice and Geneva which bolstered trade and shipping.

In 1453 the Turks gradually took control of all the islands and kept them for many centuries despite the efforts of the Venetians to retake them. Turkish occupation was particularly harsh for the areas of the Eastern Aegean and during the Greek Revolution in 1821 the islands played an active role in the naval operations of the Greeks and in return were raided and their residents slaughtered. The massacre of Hios in 1822 and that of Psara in 1824 shocked the world. The islands were finally liberated after the end of World War I. In more recent times a definitive event in their development was the Asia Minor Catastrophe of 1922 which brought large numbers of refuges to the islands.

Today thanks to the boom they experienced in the past with their trading activities and due to the numerous invaders who conquered them, the islands of the Eastern Aegean have retained a distinct identity, having taken elements from all cultures they have come into contact with. This is particularly clear in their culture and art as well as in their residential architecture. On the other hand, their natural beauty has many pleasant surprises and enchanting moments in store for the visitor, with some of the islands being verdant and others wild and barren. Yet another factor contributing to this is that these islands have never experienced the tourist development that occurred on other islands in the Aegean, making them ideal for quiet holidays close to nature and tradition.

lands. During the Peloponnesian Wars (431-404 BC) their allegiance swung between Athens and Sparta.

After the end of the war they fell into decline and in 388 BC were subjected to the Macedonians and later the Ptolemies of Egypt only to end up, much weakened, in the hands of the Romans in the 1st century BC.

The Byzantines prevailed in the area in the 4th century AD. During the Byzantine period the islands of the Eastern Aegean were a centre for maritime trade and certain

# Mytilini (Lesvos)

**HISTORY:** The oldest traces of civilization on the island date from prehistoric times (3000 BC). Around 1000 BC, it was colonized by the Aeolians, who founded several major cities, among them Mytilini. It was the homeland of numerous Greek philosophers and lyric poets (Sappho, Alkaios, Pittakos), reaching the height of its prosperity in the 7th and 6th century, after which time it shared the fate of the majority of the other Aegean islands.

Subjugated successively by the Persians, Athenians, Macedonians, Ptolemies and Romans, during the Byzantine era it fell to the Genoese adventurer Gattelusio (1354). While retaining Byzantine traditions, the island enjoyed a second period of peace and prosperity at that time, before succumbing to the Turks in 1462. Lesvos was liberated in 1912. After the Asia Minor disaster (1922) many Greek refugees established themselves here. In more recent

*Area:* 1,630 sq. km. *Population:* 88,601 *Capital:* Mytilini
*How to get there:* By air from Athens, by ship from Piraeus,
Thessaloniki, Kavala, the Cyclades, Crete, Dodecanese, Samos,
Ikaria and in the summer from Ayvalik (Turkey)

years Mytilini has experienced continuous progress and development in the arts, giving birth to Eftaliotis and the Nobel laureate Elytis, among other distinguished writers.

**SIGHTSEEING:** Mytilini owes its configuration to volcanic activity in the distant past. It is the third largest Greek island and one of the most important as far as history and a varied landscape are concerned. The famous petrified

forest is located at Sigri, where over a million years ago the tree trunks were covered with volcanic ash.

In the capital, neoclassic mansions co-exist with multistorey apartment buildings. The fortress built by Francesco Gattelusio in 1373 is one of the largest and best preserved in Greece. One can visit the Hellenistic theatre, remains of the cemetery used during the Classical, Hellenistic and Roman eras, the Archaeological Museum, the Folk Art Museum, the Roman aqueduct (2nd- 3rd c. AD) to the north of the city, to name just a few sights. Among the island's major towns are Thermi, renowned for its hot springs and Bronze Age finds (3000 BC); Mithymna also known as Molyvos, as prosperous now as it was in 2800 BC; Eressos, a little port, with a splendid beach and finds from ancient to mediaeval times housed in the local museum. Typical of the island is the local festival that takes place every year on the fourth Sunday after Easter in the chapel of

Agios Haralambos (near Agia Paraskevi), called the Festival of the Bull.

Mytilini is famous for its Byzantine monasteries and churches containing precious icons, woodcarvings and manuscripts. Generally speaking, it is a fascinating island from virtually every point of view – in terms of scenery and recreation opportunities, a place where vestiges of the past can be seen against the background of a progressive modern society. The extensive tourist facilities, fine road net-work and beach studded coast draw crowds of tourists every year.

# Chios Inousses, Psara

**HISTORY:** Chios' history begins in the distant past. Originally called Makri or Pityousa, it was colonized by the Ionians in the 8th century BC and enjoyed great power and prosperity until it succumbed to the Persians at the end of the 6th century. Athenians, Macedonians and Romans all governed the island in their turn. Its later history was similarly tumultuous with the Genoese and Venetians vying for domination after 1204 until 1344 when the Genoese secured their po-sition. Under the Giustinianis commerce flourished in Chios thanks to its monopoly of the mastic trade. In 1566 it was subjugated by the Turks who continued to give it preferential treatment until 1821. In 1822, however, they devastated the island, massacring the population: the earthquake of 1881 completed the destruction. The island was liberated in 1912. Korais and Phycharis, two outstanding figures in modern Greek letters, were born in Chios.

*Area: 842 sq. km.* **Population:** *48,700* **Capital:** *Chios*
***How to get there:*** *By plane from Athens, by ship from Piraeus, Thessaloniki, Kavala, Mytilini, Syros, the Dodecanese, Crete, the Cyclades and, in summer, Cesme (Turkey)*

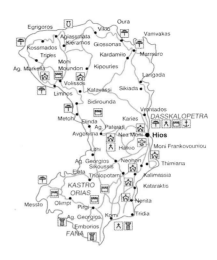

**SIGHTSEEING:** The capital, a bustling town on the east coast, has much for one to see. The old town with its Turkish neighbourhood lies within the walls of the Genoese fortress (built on 10th century Byzantine foundations). Here one can visit the palace of the Giustinianis, the tomb of Kara Ali, Byzantine monuments and the Turkish baths. Also worth visiting are the Archaeological Museum, the Art Museum, and the Korai Library with its collection of rare

manuscripts, traditional costumes and folk art. One of the major monuments on the island is Nea Moni, the 11th century monastery founded by the emperor Constantine IX the Monomachos and dedicated to the Assumption. It is one of the finest examples of Byzantine art and architecture in Greece. There are many other monasteries and churches on the island, most notably: the 7th century church of Agios Isidoros near Volissos, an important example of an early Christian basilica; Panayia of Agrelopos (14th c.) at Kalamoti; Agios Ioannis Argentis (14th c.) at Katarrakti; and the monastery of the Taxiarches also at Kalamoti. Excavations have unearthed ancient sites at Emborio, Kato Fana and Lagada. Near Vrontado, there is a monument associated with Homer who is said by some sources to have been born on Chios. Called "daskalopetra" (teaching stone), it seems, however, to have been a shrine to Cybele. Unique to Chios are the fascinating mastic villages in the south of the island. Walled settlements dating from the 14th and 15th century, whose architecture and unusual wall decorations are not found in the north of the island, exist here. Pyrgi and Mesta are the best preserved of these villages and have been declared landmarks. The northern sector is

more sparsely populated. Neolithic artifacts have been discovered at Agiasmata, where there are also hot springs.

Chios' beaches are accessible by car or by boat. Among the best are Kampos, Karfas, Kato Fana and Emborio, which has black sand. The island's facilities, historic monuments and lovely scenery are attracting more and more visitors.

**INOUSSES** *(14 sq. km., 703 inh.)* is the collective name for the islets lying to the northeast of Chios; only one of them is inhabited and there is a daily boat connection with Chios. These islands have a long naval tradition. Because of their strategic location they were a bone of contention among rival powers. Inousses has not been developed for tourism, but its lovely beaches, ship owners' villas and Naval Museum make for a pleasant sojourn.

**PSARA** *(40 sq. km., 460 inh.)* lies northwest of Chios with which it is connected daily by boat.

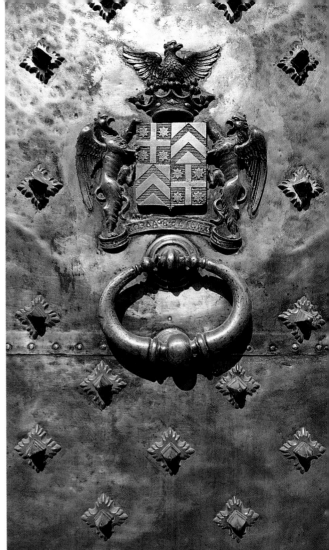

Inhabited since the Mycenaean era, its fortunes have always been bound to the sea. Its navy's feats during the War of Independence made it famous, but the Turks burned the island in retribution in 1824.

The town with its old mansions, the church of Agios Nikolaos and the monastery of Prophitis Ilias housing rare books and heirlooms are its only landmarks. One can take a caique to the island's beaches and to Antipsara opposite. There are a few inns and rooms in private houses.

# Samos

**HISTORY:** Initially joined to the Asia Minor Coast, Samos became separated from the mainland following enormous geological upheavals. According to the myth it was the birthplace of the goddess Hera. Before being colonized by the Ionians around the first millennium BC, it was inhabited by the Carians and Pelasgians. Samos enjoyed its greatest glory in the 6th and 5th century BC. Subsequently, it was dominated by the Persians during the Persian Wars, later becoming a member of the Athenian Confederacy. When Samos revolted against the alliance, the Athenians laid waste the island in revenge. It was later conquered by the Macedonians, the Ptolemies and the Romans. In 1204 it became a Frankish possession, remaining in Venetian hands until 1413, when the Genoese under the Giustinianis gained supremacy and ruled the island together

*Area: 476 sq. km. **Population:** 40,519 **Capital:** Samos or Vathy*
***How to get there:*** *By air from Athens, by ship from Piraeus, Kavala, Ikaria, Syros, Paros, Fourni, the Dodecanese, the Cyclades, Crete and Turkey, and in summer by Flying Dolphin to and from the Dodecanese*

with Chios. In 1453 with the fall of Constantinople to the Turks, the island was abandoned, its inhabitants fleeing to Chios. In the 16th century Turkish attempts to resettle Samos succeeded. The island remained under Turkish rule until 1912 when it was finally united with Greece.

**SIGHTSEEING**: The capital, Samos or Vathy, lies in the eastern part of the island. It is one of its three major ports, the other two being Karlovassi and Pythagorio. There is an archaeological museum here with local finds, plus a museum of ecclesiastical art, a fine arts museum, a Byzantine collection, folk art museum and library.

Excavations, undertaken primarily by the German School, have unearthed ruins of houses and the ancient acropolis at Pythagorio within a perimeter of approximately 6,400 metres. While the walls enclose an ancient theatre and cemetery, the most important structure is the water tunnel of Eupalinos, discovered in 1881. Other ruins near Pythagorio include a sanctuary to Hera, whose oldest section dates from the 10th century BC. In the 7th century the old temple was replaced by a new one designed by the architect Rhoikos. The largest in Greece, it was destroyed by fire in 538 BC. Other buildings in the area belong to the Hellenistic and Roman periods. Near the village of Kosmadaisi lies the cave of Pythagoras which tradition maintains was used by the great philosopher-mathematician as a refuge.

Samos possesses a host of Byzantine churches and monasteries, of which the two most important are about 25 km. from the capital. The monastery of the Holy Cross was founded in 1582, followed shortly after by that of Megali Panayia (Great Virgin). Both contain remarkable frescoes, icons and beautifully carved icon screens. Slightly older is the monastery of the Virgin Vrontiani (1566) near the village of Vourliotes. Another church, the 11th century church of Our Lady, lies near Karlovassi at Potami. Both Agios Haralambos and Our Lady Makrini, on the west coast of

the island near Kallithea, have frescoes painted in the 14th century.

Samos is ideal for excursions by boat or on foot, swimming and water sports. Kokkari, a charming seaside village with a wonderful beach, is near the capital. The northeast section of the island, near the Kotsikas peninsula, is a fun place to explore. From here one can get to the islets opposite, Makronisi and Agios Nikolaos. Boats leave from Laka for Kasonisi and from Marathokampo for Samopoula. These uninhabited islands are wonderful for bathing and picnics. The beaches at Karlovassi, Potami and all along the coast from Heraion to Psilli Ammo are perfect for swimming and water sports, while hikers and hunters will want to head for the mountains. Samos is blessed with a varied scenery, ranging from rugged mountain peaks to verdant valleys and delightful shores. Its lush environment combined with its extensive tourist facilities account for the crowds of tourists that flood it every summer.

# Ikaria Fourni

**HISTORY:** Known by many names in antiquity, the island was called Ikaria because according to myth it was here that Icarus fell into the sea and was buried. Some legends maintain that the god Dionysus was born here. Colonized by the Ionians in the 8th century BC, it later fell to the Persians. After the 4th century BC little mention is made of Ikaria in historical documents. It was ceded to Venice by the Byzantines, occupied by the Turks in 1567 and united with Greece in 1912.

**SIGHTSEEING:** Ikaria is best known for its radioactive hot springs. A small archaeological collection is housed in the high school in the capital; the finds come from ruins near Fanari, Kampos (ancient Oinoe), and Armenisti (4th and 5th c. BC tombs, temple of Artemis). One may also visit lovely Byzantine churches, monasteries and the 10th century fortress of Nikaria. It is a very mountainous islands dotted with rustic villages (Steli, Dafni) and rimmed with superb beaches (Agios Kirykos, Evdilos, Mesakti, and

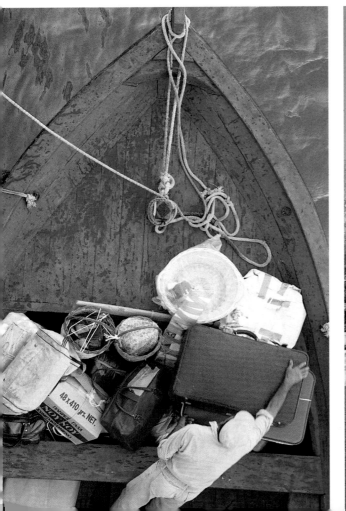

*Area:* 255 sq. km. *Population:* 7,559 **Capital:** *Agios Kirykos*
*How to get there:* By ship from Piraeus, Samos, Paros, Syros,
Fourni, Kavala, the Dodecanese, Crete and the Cyclades

many others). Though Ikaria is off the beaten track as yet, visitors will find the facilities and the road network more than adequate.

**FOURNI:** Fourni is the collective name for a group of tiny islands linked by caique with Ikaria. Despite its size (30 sq. km., pop. 1,203), it has been inhabited since ancient times. With its present population mainly engaged in fishing, Fourni is a fine place for a simple holiday close to nature.

# THE ISLANDS OF THE
# NORTHERN AEGEAN

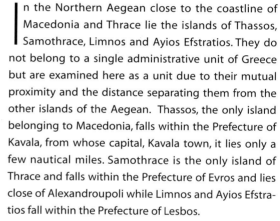

In the Northern Aegean close to the coastline of Macedonia and Thrace lie the islands of Thassos, Samothrace, Limnos and Ayios Efstratios. They do not belong to a single administrative unit of Greece but are examined here as a unit due to their mutual proximity and the distance separating them from the other islands of the Aegean. Thassos, the only island belonging to Macedonia, falls within the Prefecture of Kavala, from whose capital, Kavala town, it lies only a few nautical miles. Samothrace is the only island of Thrace and falls within the Prefecture of Evros and lies close of Alexandroupoli while Limnos and Ayios Efstratios fall within the Prefecture of Lesbos.

These are islands with a very particular physiognomy which have not experienced great tourist development like the more southerly islands of Greece, that is with the exception of Thassos. Free of the crowds of tourists which inundate the rest of the Aegean, they are ideal for those who seek peace and quiet on their holidays. Over recent years, though, there has been an increase in tourist levels, but they remain primarily a pole of attraction for the residents of Northern Greece.

Thassos is a verdant island with pines covering almost its entire surface area from its highest points right down to the sea. The combination of colours, the green of the forests and the blue of the sea, is something no visitor can forget. The crystal clear waters and the clean beaches make for images of rare beauty. Moreover, Thassos is home to unique treasures of the past since it flourished in antiquity thanks to its fertile soils, gold and silver deposits, and the trade in its famed wine.

Samothrace, home of the Cabeiri, is an exceptionally mountainous island with the highest peal being Mt. Saos at 1,800m. Swathed in greenery it is a unique haven for nature lovers being full of running water, waterfalls and wild, forest vegetation. Its archaeological monuments scattered across the entire island aptly convey to visitors the mysterious aura of another age.

Limnos, a volcanic island, was, according to tradition, the place where the god Hephaestus had his workshop. With most of the island covered in flat plains, it enchants the visitor with its simplicity and peaceful air. Its villages are picturesque, its people warm hearted and friendly and its beaches numerous and long, with clean waters and golden sands. There is no shortage of archaeological monuments on the island, witnesses to the island's rich historical past. Apart from the marvellous exhibits in the archaeological museum of the island's capital, Myrina, the village of Poliochnis is of particular interest dating back to the 4th millennium BC.

At a distance of 18 miles south of Limnos is the islet of Ayios Efstratios, also volcanic; a deserted, virgin island, once a place of exile and ideal for those who seek quietude even today.

# Thassos

**HISTORY:** The Thracians are considered to have been the first inhabitants of the island in around 3500 BC. They were eventually succeeded by the Phoenicians and by Parian colonists (7th c. BC). Civilization in Thassos reached its peak in the 6th century; from the 5th century on it was vanquished by the Persians, Athenians, Spartans, Macedonians and Romans. During the Byzantine era pirate raids alternated with occupation by foreign powers (Franks, Turks, Russians) to disrupt the island. Thassos was liberated and united with Greece in 1913.

**SIGHTSEEING:** On the north side of the island, the capital –occupies the site of the ancient city (7th c. BC). Excavations by the French School have brought to light a good many buildings of that era (agora, sanctuary, theatre, etc.); the smaller finds may be seen in the local archaeological museum. A good road network permits the visitor to travel easily to the island's 20 villages and fine beaches. Each village has its own relic from antiquity or from Byzantium. Near Panayia there is the Dracotrypa (Dragon's Lair) Cave inhabited in ancient

*Area:* 379 sq. km. *Population:* 13,111
*Capital:* Thassos (Limenas)
*How to get there:* By boat from Kavala or Keramoti.

times, while the ancient city of Ainyra is located near Potamia. The coast of Thassos is full of contrasts: serene and placid to the west and north, sandy beaches surrounded by greenery to the east, rocky and steep to the south (Chrysi Ammoudia, Alyki, Limenaria, etc.). Thassos is a wooded island with a varied landscape and a variety of tourist facilities, all of which have made it much in demand in the last few years.

# Samothrace

**HISTORY:** Inhabited since the second millennium BC by pre-Greek tribes, the island was settled by Thracian, Ionian and Aeolian colonists who merged together to create a brilliant civilization. Its history is interwoven with that of the Sanctuary of the Great Gods and the presence of the Kabeirian Mysteries, which stood out during the Classical and Hellenistic era as one of the major pan Hellenic and international religious centres of the times. During the Middle Ages it fell into decline and little is known of it during the Turkish Occupation. Samothrace was united with Greece in 1912.

**SIGHTSEEING:** The hamlet of Palaiopolis lies near the site of the ancient capital and the Sanctuary of the Great Gods. Here ruins of the ancient temple have been found, the Anaktoron (hall of initiation) and other extraordinary things, such as the famous Winged Victory (dedicated by the Rhodians to the temple) now in the Louvre. The local museum has a

*Area:* 178 sq. km. ***Population:*** 2,871 ***Capital:*** Samothrace
***How to get there:*** By ship from Alexadroupolis,
Kavala and Limnos

fine collection of ancient objects. The capital is a traditional settlement located in the interior of the island. Therma offers a marvelous view and hot springs, while Ammos is a wonderful beach nestled among thick greenery and watered by a brook.

Though it has so much to offer, Samothrace has not been developed for tourism and remains off the beaten track, a perfect spot for a peaceful holiday.

# Limnos Agios Efstratios

**HISTORY:** The Thracians were the first to settle on the island in Neolithic times; by the Bronze Age a prosperous civilization had emerged. By the 5th century Limnos had fallen under Athenian influence, and was subsequently governed by the Macedonians and then the Romans. In later years it belonged to Byzantium, Venice and the Ottoman Empire, being united with Greece in 1912.

**SIGHTSEEING:** Myrina, which has retained its ancient name, is located near the ancient city where statuettes and inscriptions have been found. There were several important cities on the island in antiquity – Hephaistia, inhabited since prehistoric times; Kabeirio, with its age-old sanctuary; Poliochni. One can visit the beaches and villages of Moudros, Livadohori, Thanos, Skandali, and Kaminia by either car or boat, and there are plenty of hotels and rooms for rent to accommodate the large number of tourists who are beginning to know this picturesque island.

*Area: 476 sq. km. **Population:** 15,721 **Capital:** Myrina (Kastro)*
***How to get there:*** *By air from Athens, Thessaloniki, Mytilini;*
*by ship from Piraeus, Kavala, Euboea, Agios Konstantinos,*
*Mytilini, the Cyclades, the Dodecanese, Crete.*

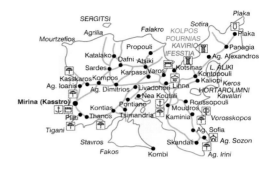

**AGIOS EFSTRATIOS:** This little island (43 sq. km., pop. 296) is linked by ship with Limnos, Kavala, Euboea, Alexandroupolis, Samothrace and Mytilini. It is surrounded by lovely, unspoiled beaches, accessible by foot or caique. Its chapels, caves and a few remnants from antiquity are the only sights to see. It has virtually no tourist amenities and is recommended for those who wish to experience genuine island life in quiet surroundings.

# THE DODECANESE

The group of islands called the Dodecanese lie in the eastern Aegean, being bounded on the east by the coast of Asia Minor, on the west by the Cyclades, on the north by Samos and Ikaria and on the south by Crete. Although the name means 'twelve islands', the group actually consists of 14 islands and some 80 rocky islets, most of them uninhabited. The most important islands are Patmos, Leros, Kalymnos, Kos, Nisyros, Astypalaia, Tilos, Syme, Chalki, Rhodes, Kastellorizo, Karpathos and Kasos.

Thanks to their position close to Asia and in the direction of Africa, the Dodecanese have often been the target of marauders, and their history has been a troubled one. In the fifteenth century BC, the first Achaean settlers arrived, probably from Crete, though they were later driven out by Dorian invaders. The Dorians fostered the development of the islands, which by the seventh century BC had founded colonies to the east and west. In the Persian Wars, most of the Dodecanese islands came under Persian control, and fought on their side against the other Greeks. After the Greek victory at the battle of Salamis in 480 BC, however, the islanders were able to shake off the Persian yoke. After this time, each island followed its own course through history down to the Middle Ages. The Dodecanese played an important part in the history of the Crusades, since many of the island harbours were used as operational bases. After 1204, the islands formed an independent state, with Leo Gavalas as its prince, and in 1250 they were ruled directly by the Emperor of Nicaea, which was the rump Byzantine state. In 1303, Kasos and Karpathos were taken by Andreas Cornaros of Crete, and in 1306 Rhodes, Kos and Leros were sold to the Knights Templar of St John, whose

realm ultimately extended to include Chalki, Syme, Tilos and Kalymnos as well. In 1522, the Turks drove out the Knights of St John and established themselves, granting the islands many privileges and a considerable degree of autonomy. In 1912 the Dodecanese islands were occupied by Italy, not being finally annexed to Greece until 1946-1948.

The most northerly of the Dodecanese is Patmos, the holy island of the Revelation. It was there that St John the Divine composed his prophetic book, in a cave which can still be seen today. Above the chief town of Patmos towers the monastery of St John the Divine, fortified by a strong wall. It was founded in 1088 and is one of the most important treasures of Byzantine art, with superb wall-paintings, icons, ecclesiastical relics and a library with important manuscripts and codices.

Leros is an attractive and fertile island which is ideal for quiet holidays. Kalymnos, the island of sponge-fishers, is mountainous and rocky and can boast only one stretch of flat land, though this is very fertile.

Kos, the island where the great physician Hippocrates was born in the fifth century BC, combines natural beauty with numerous important ancient monuments. In the chief town are remains of the ancient city: the port, the agora, the sanctuary of Aphrodite Pandemos (2nd century BC), the stadium, Roman baths, stoas, a gymnasium (2nd century BC), Hellenistic and

Roman houses with fine mosaic ornamentation, and the superb Casa Romana, now restored, dating from the second century BC. Also to be seen is the castle of the Knights of St John, where there is an open-air museum. Of particular interest is the archaeological museum of Kos, which has an excellent collection of sculptures, most of them dating from the Hellenistic and Roman periods. Very close to the main town is the archaeological site of the Asclepium of Kos (Hellenistic period), with the ruins of the most important centre for early Greek medicine.

The volcanic island of Nisyros is a place of unique beauty. In the centre of the island is a

volcanic crater with a diameter of 4 km. Astypalaia, too, is of volcanic origin, consisting of two pieces of land joined by a narrow isthmus. The deeply-indented shoreline means that there are plenty of idyllic bays for swimming. Above the natural amphitheatre which is the site of the island's chief town towers a thirteenth century Venetian castle.

Tilos, sparsely-populated and off the tourist trail, is a tiny paradise of dense vegetation and plentiful streams.

Syme is a barren island close to the shore of Asia Minor. The chief town is crowned with the castle dating from the time of the Knights of St John, and is notable for its many neo-Classical houses. There are Byzantine churches all over the island, whose patron saint is St Michael: his church (18th century) at Panormitis Bay attracts many pilgrims to the island.

Chalki is the smallest inhabited island in the Dodecanese, but even so the terrain of the island is highly varied. In antiquity, it was known for its copper mines, to which it owes its name ('chalkos' = copper). Among the picturesque houses of the chief town stands the church of St Nicholas, with its bell-tower, while above Chora, the old capital, a medieval castle stands atop a steep cliff.

The most important and largest of the Dodecanese islands is Rhodes, which thanks to its great natural beauty and the wealth of its historical past has been highly developed for tourism. Rhodes is among the most cosmopolitan islands in the Mediterranean. The three ancient cities of the island are of great archaeological interest. Lindos, where today there is an attractive village and a fine beach, preserves ruins of the Hellenistic sanctuary and temple of Athena Lindia (c. 330 BC). The acropolis of ancient Ialysos has come to light on Mt Philerimos, with traces of a prehistoric settlement in the immediate vicinity. The third of the Doric cities of Rhodes was Kameiros, where a temple of Athena has been discovered together with numerous houses. In 408 BC, these cities united to found a new capital on the north side of the island: Rhodes itself. Most of the surviving traces of ancient Rhodes are to be seen on Monte Smith hill (the acropolis, the theatre, the stadium, the temples of Apollo and Athena). The picturesque old town of Rhodes, on the other hand, reflects the medieval history of the island. The entire town is surrounded by impressive walls dating from the time of the Knights of St John, while within it, restored by the Italians, are many buildings of the same period and the imposing Palace of the Grand Master. The port of Rhodes (Mandraki), straddled according to tradition by the famous bronze statue of the Colossus, is a place of unique interest, with the Tower of St Nicholas, the old windmills and the statues of two deer on high pillars along its seafront. Interesting buildings from the period of Italian rule are to be seen in the area around Mandraki, while the monuments of the Byzantine and Turkish periods give the old town an atmosphere all its own. The entire past of Rhodes and the history of its achievements in the arts (with the main emphasis on the Hellenistic period) is to be seen in the archaeological museum, housed in the Hospital

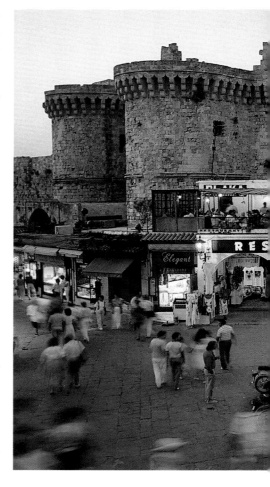

of the Knights. The modern city has tourist amenities of all kinds, and the island of Rhodes is packed with sites and places of great beauty and interest.

To the east of Rhodes lies Kastellorizo, an idyllic spot which is ideal for quiet holidays. Excavations on the island have brought to light the ruins of a Mycenean settlement, and the numerous finds dating from the historic period are housed in a small archaeological museum. The chief town is lent added picturesqueness by its whitewashed houses, whose multicoloured doors and windows are reflected in the waters of the harbour.

Although Karpathos is large in terms of size, it is barren, isolated and depopulated. This is perhaps why some very old traditions have managed to survive down to the present day. In the village of Olympos, for example, the local people use a dialect in which there are traces of the Doric tongue. Karpathos has the remains of three ancient cities, and at Pigadi (ancient Poseidio) there is a private collection whose finds cover the period from the Mycenean period down to Hellenistic times.

Kasos, the most southerly island in the Dodecanese, is not often visited by tourists. It is a mountainous island, with a rocky coast, and the few beaches are close to the main town (Fri) and the port of Emborio.

Today the Dodecanese, Greece's most remote islands, rely on agriculture, fisheries, sponge fishing and utilization of the mineral wealth they have in significant quantities since they are volcanic islands. Of course, on most the main wealth-generating source is tourism. Nonetheless, there is no uniformity in economic terms among the Dodecanese and each island has gone down on its own individual path. The administrative and economic centre of the Dodecanese is Rhodes.

# Rhodes

**HISTORY:** The archaeological finds and some of the place names in Rhodes indicate that the island's first inhabitants were pre-Hellenic tribes related to the peoples of Asia Minor. The Achaeans settled here in the second millennium BC and gave rise to what is known as the Aegean civilization. They were succeeded by the Dorians, who founded three cities (Lindos, Ialyssos and Kameiros) and were extremely active in developing colonies and commerce. Their prosperity reached its peak in the 4th century BC. It was at this time that the Lindos sculptor Chares created one of the seven wonders of the ancient world – the Colossus of Rhodes- destroyed by an earthquake in 222 BC. Rhodes attempted to resist the Macedonians and later gave full support to the Romans. During the Middle Ages, many powers laid claim to this rich island, including the Arabs (7th c.), the Saracens (8th c.) and

*Area:* 1,398 sq. km. *Population:* 87,831 *Capital:* Rhodes
*How to get there:* By air from Athens, European capitals,
Crete, Mykonos, Kos, Karpathos, Leros, Kassos;
by ship from Piraeus, the Cyclades, Crete and the Dodecanese

the Crusaders (1097), not to mention the number of pirates. In 1306, the Order of the Knights of St. John of Jerusalem took control over the island, which was administered by the Grand Masters who also built the medieval city and fortress. Their rule lasted until 1552 when they succumbed to the Turks. Rhodes was governed by the Italians from 1912 to 1945; the Dodecanese were restored to Greece in 1947.

**SIGHTSEEING:** At the crossroads of civilization, Rhodes with its age-old history and its formidable natural beauty was and still is a major pole of attraction. Of great interest from the archaeological standpoint, its three ancient cities command the most attention. Lindos, the most important, is also blessed with a lovely beach and a charming village. On the acropolis one can see ruins of the temple of Athena in the southwest section of Rhodes. Its acropolis stands on the peak of Mt. Philerimos and contains the foundations of the temple of Athena Ialyssia as well as Mycenaean tombs. In the valley below, a necropolis with tombs from the Late Mycenaean to the Classical periods lies near a Doric fountain and ruined early Christian Lindia, the Doric stoa, palaces etc. Kameiros, an unfortified city, lies on the northwest coast of the island. Among its ruins one can find a temple of Athena, a stoa, an aqueduct and a number of graves in which consider-

able jewellery, pottery, sculpture and inscriptions were discovered. Lalyssos, the third, was one of the oldest cities and Byzantine churches.

The capital with 30,000 inhabitants is a modern town equipped with all the amenities. The walls of the castle of the Knights separates the new city from the old – one of the most evocative places in Greece, with its flagged streets, arched facades, quaint houses, minarets, and myriad shops and restaurants. The northern

district belonged exclusively to the Knights. This is where they built the Palace of the Grand Master (now a museum) and the inns of the various tongues or language groups. Interesting monuments are not absent from the modern town either, where multi-storey hotels stand next to neo-Gothic administration buildings watched over by old windmills. Rhodes also possesses one of the finest aquariums in the Mediterranean, where the life of the deep is depicted in a particularly fascinating manner. The outskirts of the town are embellished by a large public park called Rodini with artificial canals and a small zoo. From the hill named Monte Smith inside the town limits there is a panoramic view of the whole island; modern-day residents have chosen to build their pretty villas on this pine-covered hill where the acropolis once stood.

Twelve kilometres from the capital, the seaside village of Kallithea is an organized spa with mineral water to drink and bathe in.

The phenomenon of the Valley of the Butterflies can be enjoyed from July to the end of August. The vision of thousands of iridescent

butterflies hovering over the fields is unforgettable, but even without them the scenery
makes an indelible impression on memory.

Rhodes also offers an abundance of Byzantine
monuments. In the town, the ones worth noting
are: are the 5th century basilica, Panayia of the
Kastro (11th-12th c.), Agios Georgios (14th c.)
and Agios Phanourios (13th c.). Further afield, at
Philerimos, lies Our Lady of Philerimos (15th c.),
while near the village of Lardos two monasteries
are worth a visit: Psenis with its important wall
paintings and the now abandoned Skiathis.

Rhodes is considered among the most sophisticated islands in the Mediterranean. Its hotels
– of every category – are superb – nightclubs,
discos, bars, a gambling casino and theatres –
in the town. Conversely, the less densely settled southern part of the island is the place to
go for more relaxing holidays, picturesque villages and tranquil beaches.

Rhodes may be different from the other Greek
islands, but its cosmopolitan atmosphere, rich
history and wealth of exquisite monuments
are some of the features that make it so individual and delightful.

# Karpathos

**HISTORY:** Little is known about the early history of the island. In antiquity, its three cities belonged to the Athenian League. From the 3rd century BC, it was under the domination of Rhodes and shared the larger island's fate. The Middle Ages were disastrous for Karpathos; it was a Frankish possession until 1312, falling to the Venetians in the 16th century, when the Turks took over. Like the rest of the Dodecanese, it was occupied by the Italians from 1912 till the end of the war and united with Greece in 1947.

**SIGHTSEEING:** The village of Valada divides the island into two unequal sections – the long, narrow part that contains the Pano Horia (Upper Villages) and the flattish southern district with its Kato Horia (Lower Villages). The capital lies in the southern portion, its modern houses built on the site of ancient Poseidion. Among the Kato Horia, the most important are Arkasa, identified with the ancient Arkesia whose ruins stand high on the hill above; Menetes, founded in the Middle Ages; Aperi, the administrative centre

*Area:* 301 sq. km. *Population:* 4,645 *Capital:* Karpathos (Pigadia)
*How to get there:* By air from Athens, Rhodes, Crete, Kassos;
by ship from Piraeus, Crete, the Cyclades
and the rest of the Dodecanese

since 1892; and Odos, where there is a folk art museum. The northern section contains the island's most interesting and most important village, Olympos or Elympos (10th or 15th century), whose centuries-old customs, traditions and dialect render it a living museum. One can get there via caique from Diafani. The unspoiled beaches, the locals' hospitality and traditional way of life make Karpathos a pleasant place to spend a holiday.

# Kassos

**HISTORY:** Kassos is the southern most island in the Dodecanese and is situated very close to Karpathos, with which it shares a common history. It was first settled by the Phoenicians and shared the fate of its neighbours until the 13th century AD. Ruled by the family Cornaro of Venice, it submitted to the Turks in the 16th century and suffered its greatest destruction during the Turkish occupation: in 1824, the Turkish-Egyptian fleet burnt and laid waste the whole island. It was united with Greece in 1947.

**SIGHTSEEING:** A predominantly mountainous island, Kassos has an interesting interior which will reward exploration. In the capital, Fry, built on the Gulf of Bouka, there are a number of old mansions and the local museum has a collection of both archaeological artifacts and folk art. The main attractions are the Sellai cave with its stalactites, the churches and the ruined fortresses in the villages of Agia Marina, Polis (the old capital), Emboreio and Panayia, as well as the charming hamlet

*Area:* 66 sq. km. *Population:* 1,184 *Capital:* Fry (Orfys)
*How to get there:* By boat from Piraeus,
Crete and the rest of the Dodecanese

of Arvanitohori, nestled in the island's only green valley. The coasts of Kassos are rocky and steep, the few beaches being near Fry and Emboreio. A picturesque island with very little tourist development, Kassos has a few rooms to rent for its occasional visitors.

# Symi

**HISTORY:** The island, where according to tradition the Three Graces were born, has been inhabited since prehistoric times. The first settlers were the Lelegians. Later, sharing the history of the rest of the Dodecanese, it witnessed a succession of conquerors (Argives, Rhodians, Romans, Byzantines). Under the rule of the Knights of St. John for about two centuries, it fell to the Turks in 1522. Thanks to its location along important trade routes, Symi began to develop economically. Symi was under Italian occupation from 1912 to 1945; it was here that the protocol ceding the Dodecanese to the Allies was signed at the end of the war.

**SIGHTSEEING:** The capital of the island has retained all its neo-classical elegance. Dominated by the castle of the Knights, it is divided into Ano (Upper) Symi (Hora) and the lower town (Yialo). Symi is noted for its long tradition in wood carving, and beautiful examples can still be seen in the island's houses. There

*Area:* 58 sq. km. *Population:* 2,273 *Capital:* Symi
*How to get there:* By ship from Piraeus, Crete, Samos, Rhodes and the rest of the Dodecanese

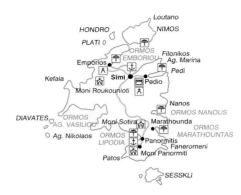

are also a number of exquisite churches and monasteries containing fine carvings and mosaics, as, for example, the Megali Panayia of the Kastro, the monasteries of the Archangel Michael Panormites, Megalos Sotiras, and others. Caiques are available to take one to the picturesque beaches (Nanou, Marathounta) and neighbouring islets. Generally speaking, Symi has undergone little tourist development as yet and is a fine place for those in search of peace and quiet.

# Halki

**HISTORY:** According to myth Halki was initially the dwelling place of the Titans, who were succeeded by Pelasgians, Carians, Dorians and Phoenicians. The island enjoyed great prosperity in antiquity (10th-5th c. BC), taking its name from the copper mines once so productive here. From the Hellenistic period on, its history was similar to that of the neighbouring islands; it witnessed a series of conquerors before being united with Greece in 1947.

**SIGHTSEEING:** Although small, Halki has an extremely varied landscape; it has steep mountains and fertile valleys, rugged shores and serene beaches. In the capital, built up the sides of a mountain, the bell tower of Agios Nikolaos and the windmills stand out from the background of dazzling white houses. While in the old capital, Hora, right in the middle of the island, one can see the church of Panayia along with ruins of the ancient

*Area:* 28 sq. km. *Population:* 334 *Capital:* Halki (Nimborio)
*How to get there:* By ship from Rhodes, Piraeus
and the rest of the Dodecanese

acropolis and the mediaeval castle. Other
sights include the monasteries of Ai Yiannis,
Agia Triada, Stavros and the Archangel
Michael. The beaches are accessible on foot
or by boat and caiques are also available to
cross over to the nearby islet of Alimnia.
Though little frequented and lacking amenities, Halki offers the visitor a taste of what
genuine island life is like off the beaten path.

# Tilos

**HISTORY:** Ruined courses of Pelasgian walls are evidence that the first inhabitants of the island were most probably Pelasgians, who were followed by Dorian settlers. However, even before these tribes had appeared, the island was home to a species of prehistoric elephant judging from skeletons found in the Harmadio cave. During the Classical period, Tilos founded colonies in Sicily, but its subsequent history was identical to that of its neighbours.

**SIGHTSEEING:** The capital, Megalo Horio, lies in the interior of the island. There are sections of an ancient wall interspersed between its houses. Its ancient necropolis contains quite a number of graves. More recent ruins are the castle of the Knights on the hill above the town and a Venetian tower, located in the centre of the island, near Micro Horio. The two ports, Plaka and Livadia, are charming, picturesque villages fronted by pleasant beach-

*Area: 63 sq. km. Population: 301 Capital: Megalo Horio*
*How to get there: By ship from Piraeus, Amorgos,*
*Crete and the rest of the Dodecanese*

es. Among other sights on the island are the numerous churches and monasteries, some of which are decorated with fine frescoes (Taxiarches, Agios Panteleimonas, Agios Antonios). All the beaches on Tilos, of which the most beautiful is Erystos, may be reached either on foot or by caique; few are accessible by car. Despite its rich history, Tilos has little tourist development and will appeal to those in search of something different.

# Nissyros

**HISTORY:** Known from mythology, Nissyros is mentioned in the Homeric epics as having participated in the Trojan War. Its history throughout the ages was linked to that of its larger neighbours. The Knights of St. John assumed control over the island in the 14th century, erecting their castle in 1315. In 1947 it was united with Greece along with the rest of the Dodecanese.

**SIGHTSEEING:** An island of rare natural beauty with a serene atmosphere, Nissyros is ideal for peaceful holidays. The most impressive sight on the island is the crater of the extinct volcano at Lakki, to which the hot sulphurous springs at Loutra and Emborio owe their existence. In the capital, presided over by the castle of the Knights, sections of the ancient wall and the cemetery may be seen. The houses, either white or brightly painted, stand in utter contrast to the

*Area: 41 sq. km.* ***Population:*** *916* ***Capital:*** *Mandraki*
***How to get there:*** *By ship from Piraeus,*
*Crete and the rest of the Dodecanese*

gray volcanic rock surrounding them. Within the castle walls there is the church of Panayia Spilianis, built in 1600, which is connected with numerous local traditions. In addition to the beaches near Mandraki, there are beaches all around the island, accessible on foot or by caique; the black sand beach at Hochlaki is particularly distinctive. Possessing few facilities for tourists, Nissyros offers little in the way of amenities but much that is beautiful to its visitors.

# Kos

**HISTORY:** According to the myth, Kos was the homeland of the Giants. It was settled during the Neolithic era by the Carians, Phoenicians, Pelasgians and later by the Dorians. Along with Halikarnassos, Knidos, Lindos, Lalyssos and Kameiros, it was a member of the Dorian Hexapolis formed in 700BC. The city of Kos was founded in the 4th century BC, and it remained the centre of island life until the 6th century AD, when it was destroyed by an earthquake. Many great personalities of the ancient world claimed Kos as their birthplace: Hippocrates and Pythagoras are but two of the best known. After the decline of Rome, Kos began to prosper again in the Middle Ages. The Knights of St. John controlled the island from the 14th century until the Turkish conquest in 1522. Held by the Turks until 1912, when it passed to the Italians; it was united with Greece in 1947. The modern city was rebuilt after the devastating earthquake of 1933.

*Area: 290 sq. km. **Population:** 20,350 **Capital:** Kos*
***How to get there:*** *By air from Athens, Rhodes, Leros and Mykonos; by ship from Piraeus, the Cyclades, the northern and southern Aegean islands, the Dodecanese, Crete and Cyprus*

**SIGHTSEEING:** The third largest island of the Dodecanese group, after Rhodes and Karpathos, Kos has a large number of archaeological sites and monuments from every era. In the capital several ruins of the ancient city – temples, stoas, the agora – were discovered under the mediaeval constructions erected by the Knights of St. John around the harbour. Here, too, the plane tree which tradition maintains was planted by Hippocrates and under

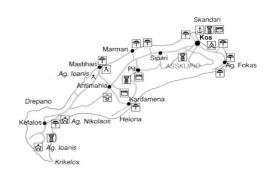

whose shade he taught his disciples still stands. The interesting finds and mosaics unearthed here are exhibited in the Archaeological Museum. One of the most important ancient sites in Kos is the Asklepeio with its temple of Asklepios, southwest of town. Other sites are at Pyli where there is a Classical temple and at Kefalo which boasts a theatre and archaic temples.

The major monuments from the time of the Knights are found in town and near Kardamaina, where there is a large Venetian castle whose walls are virtually intact. Byzantine churches still stand both in the town and in most of the villages. Kos has two ports, one in town and the other at Mastichari. It is a lush island with pretty coastal villages (Tigaki, Agios Fokas, Kardamaina), health spas (Thermes, Kardamaina), and wonderful beaches. Equipped with abundant facilities for tourists, it can offer all the amenities and is a fine spot for a pleasant, carefree holiday. Many of its beaches provide other water sports besides swimming, while at its hotels one can choose between a cosmopolitan or genuine Greek ambience, depending on one's preference.

# Astypalea

**HISTORY:** Archaeological finds show that the island was first settled by Carians long before the age of written history and that it knew great prosperity in antiquity. Otherwise, it seems to have shared the fate of the rest of the Dodecanese, experiencing both Roman and Byzantine rule. Claimed by Venice in 1207, it fell to the Turks in 1540. It was occupied by the Italians from 1912 to 1945 and united with Greece two years later.

**SIGHTSEEING:** The capital, built like an amphitheatre up the slopes of a steep hill topped by the 13th century Venetian castle, is in itself the island's chief monument. The picture is completed by the windmills standing to the south of the town. Astypalea boasts one of the loveliest churches in the Dodecanese –Panayia Portaitissa, and there are two other beautiful churches in the fortress. In the 9th century, the Byzantine castle of Agios Ioannis

*Area:* 97 sq. km. *Population:* 1,030 *Capital:* Astypalea
*How to get there:* By ship from Piraeus, the Cyclades,
Crete and the rest of the Dodecanese

was built on the west side of the island, while to the east the important monastery of Panayia Poulariani can be seen. Consisting of two sections joined by an isthmus, Astypalea is a sparsely settled island with little tourism. It has thus retained its genuine Greek atmosphere, and this plus its splendid, spotless beaches and the uninhabited islets nearby, which can be reached by caique, are good reasons for choosing the island for a restful, relaxing holiday.

# Patmos Lipsi

**HISTORY:** Apart from the mythological reference to Patmos as the place where Orestes sought refuge from the pursuit of the Furies, little is known about the early history of the island. According to archaeological evidence, it appears to have been inhabited since at least the 6th century BC. During the Hellenistic era and afterwards, it served as a place of exile, and it was here that St. John the Theologian was banished (95-97 AD) and wrote the Book of Revelations. Until the 11th century, frequent pirate raids left the island virtually deserted. But subsequently under the Byzantine and Venetian rule, Patmos began to prosper economically and culturally. In the late 17th century the celebrated Theological College was founded. Like the rest of the Dodecanese, Patmos was governed by Italy until 1945 after the Turkish defeat of 1912.

*Area:* 34 sq. km. *Population:* 2,534 *Capital:* Patmos (Hora)
*How to get there:* By ship from Piraeus, Crete, Samos
and the rest of the Dodecanese

**SIGHTSEEING:** Patmos, is one of the smallest inhabited islands in the Aegean. It possesses two principal settlements: Skala, the main port since 1600, whose snow-white houses form a semi-circle around the sea; and the capital, Patmos or Hora, perched on a hill 3 kilometres to the south. Here the houses are more impressive; many of them are grand neoclassical mansions. The most important monument on the island is situated in the central, highest point in Hora. This is the monastery-fortress of

St. John the Theologian founded in 1088. A Byzantine construction surrounded by crenellated walls, it contains one of the finest libraries in Greece, noted for its collection of rare manuscripts. The Theasury, too, has a wealth of valuable icons and liturgical vessels. Between the two main villages lies the Cave of the Apocalypse, where the sacred text was composed. On Kastelli hill, near Skala, vestiges of the acropolis and the ancient cemetery may be seen.

A few tiny hamlets, their diminished populations due to the stony soil, are scattered about the island. There is, however, an abundance of lovely, quiet beaches, some sandy, some rather rocky (Kathisma tou Apollo, Grikas, Kallikatsou, Livadi Kaloyiron, Diakofti). The easiest way to reach them is by caiques, which also make trips to the neighbouring islets of Arki and Agathonisi. Despite daily visits by cruise ships, Patmos has surprisingly little tourist development and is a good place for a peaceful holiday.

Lipsi is a cluster of tiny islands lying between Patmos and Leros, covering a total area of 16 sq. km. with 574 inhabitants. Its marvelous beaches and relaxed ways make Lipsi a sanctuary for those seeking to "get away from it all" and "go back to nature".

# Kalymnos Telendos, Pserimos

**HISTORY:** The Carians, who established themselves here in prehistoric times, were succeeded by the Dorians (ca. 1000 BC). The island later developed a distinguished civilization, influenced by Crete and linked historically with Kos. After the Roman and Byzantine periods, it was ruled by the Venetians (1204), the Knights of St. John (14th c.), the Turks (1522) and the Italians (1912) until it was united with Greece in 1947.

**SIGHTSEEING:** Podia, inhabited since antiquity, became the island's capital in 1850. Up to then the principal settlement had been Horio (Village), and remnants of Byzantine and Venetian rule can still be seen there. Northwest of Podia stands the Venetian castle of Chrysoheria, while ruins of earlier eras have been discovered at numerous points around the island (Damos, Vathy, etc.). Kalymnos is famous for its caves – the Cave of the Seven Virgins (Epta Parthenes), Skalies and Kefalos,

*Area: 111 sq. km. Population: 14,295 Capital: Kalymnos (Podia)*
*How to get there: By ship from Piraeus, the Cyclades,*
*Crete and the rest of the Dodecanese*

as well as for the church of Christ of Jerusalem (6th c.). Apart from ancient and medieval monuments, its fertile valleys and lovely beaches, Kalymnos offers the possibility of visiting its two neighbours: Telendos, which was united with Kalymnos until the earthquake of 535 AD; and Pserimos, with its exquisite beaches, a haven of tranquility. Scarcely developed for tourism, all three islands hold out a promise of picturesque and peaceful holidays.

# Leros

**HISTORY:** According to archaeological evidence, Leros has been inhabited continuously since the Neolithic era and enjoyed particular prosperity up to the Roman conquest. After that time, it shared the fate of its neighbours, being sold to the Knights of St. John (1316), subjugated by the Turks (1522) and occupied by the Italians (1912), who transformed it into a naval base. As a result, Leros was heavily bombarded during World War II.

**SIGHTSEEING:** Agia Marina is a traditional settlement displaying local architecture and a number of neoclassical mansions. It is dominated by the castle of the Knights, which occupies the site of the ancient acropolis and was inhabited until the 18th century. Here the church of Panayia of the Kastro may be seen, backed by picturesque windmills. Lakki, the island's main harbour, is known for its carefully planned layout, a heritage of the Italians. Ruins

*Area:* 53 sq. km. **Population:** 8,127 **Capital:** Agia Marina
**How to get there:** By air from Athens, Kos, Rhodes; by the ship
from Piraeus, the Cyclades, Crete and the rest of the Dodecanese

of another ancient acropolis, belonging to the 4th century have also been found on Palaiokastro hill. Because of its pleasant tree-filled villages (Partheni, Alinda, Merika) near the sea and its clean beaches easily reached by caique or car, Leros is a fine place to spend a comfortable holiday despite the constantly increasing number of visitors.

# Kastellorizo

**HISTORY:** Kastellorizo lies a mere 1.5 nautical miles from the coast of Asia Minor, from whence its first inhabitants arrived in prehistoric times. It was later settled by the Dorians and its subsequent history is linked with that of Rhodes. Over the centuries it was occupied by the Romans, the Knights of St. John, the Egyptians, the Turks and the Italians, suffering countless pirate raids in addition until its ultimate union with Greece in 1947.

**SIGHTSEEING:** Excavations have revealed Cyclopean walls and tools of the prehistoric and the Mycenaean eras, while up on the plateau of Agios Georgios a gold Mycenaean wreath (now in the Athens Archaeological Museum) was found. There were also fortified acropolises at the site of the present-day capital and Palaiokastro. The capital with its white houses and brightly coloured doors and windows presents a captivating, picturesque picture. Other sights include the 14th century castle of the Knights and a number of interesting churches: Agios Konstantinos (1833), Agios

*Area: 9 sq. km. Population: 222 Capital: Kastellorizo*
*How to get there: By ship once a week from Piraeus and twice*
*weekly from Rhodes and the rest of the Dodecanese (in summer)*

Nikolaos (11th c.), Our Lady of the Fields (17th
c.), and Agios Georgios with its catacombs.
Kastellorizo also possesses the largest and
most beautiful sea-cave in Greece, Parasta's
Cave or Phokeale (Refuge of the Seals). It is
best visited in the early evening when the
cave's waters turn astonishing shades of blue.
Caiques are available for excursions to beaches round the island and the nearby islets of Ro
and Strongyli. In addition to its delightful surroundings, Kastellorizo can promise its guests
a pleasant and tranquil stay.

# CRETE

Crete, a place of unique beauty, is the largest Greek island and the fifth-largest in the Mediterranean. It forms the southernmost extremity of Greece, and constitutes a bridge for communications between Europe and Africa.

According to the myths, Crete was the birthplace of Zeus, the primus inter pares of the Olympian gods. By Europa, Zeus fathered Minos, the mythical king of the island, who in turn gave his name to the Minoan civilisation, the oldest on the European continent. In the palace of Minos, known as the Labyrinth and designed by the architect Daedalus, lived the Minotaur, a monster with the body of a man and the head of a bull. The Minotaur is connected with the myth of the Athenian hero Theseus, who succeeded in killing the monster with the help of Ariadne, daughter of Minos. Thus he released the Athenians from the tribute of blood (seven youths and seven maidens, fed to the Minotaur) which the city had been obliged to pay to Minos.

These myths tell us much about the power which Crete had acquired in prehistoric times, as also confirmed beyond any doubt by archaeological finds.

Crete was first inhabited in the Neolithic era, but the most brilliant period in its history was the Bronze Age. Archaeologists distinguish four phases in Minoan history, in line with the founding and destruction of the Minoan palaces.

In the Pre-Palace period (2600-2000 BC), the island escaped from the isolation of the Neolithic era and began to develop in every possible way, heralding the progress to be made in later centuries. It was at this

time that the Minoans adopted a hieroglyphic script.

In the Early Palace period (2000-1700 BC), the first Minoan palaces were built at Knossos, Phaestos, Malia and Zakro. These were labyrinthine structures around which the entire settlement was organised and in which all its wealth was kept. The religious needs of the Cretans were served by shrines on the peaks of mountains. A vast quantity of finds from this period has come to light, and they impress us with the skill and delicacy of their manufacture.

In 1700 BC, a severe earthquake badly damaged the island, but in the Late Palace period (1700-1450 BC), new and equally magnificent palaces were built at Knossos, Phaestos, Malia, Zakro and Kydonia (Chania). These luxurious royal palaces contained the apartments of the king (with wall-paintings), shrines, 'washing tanks' for use during rites of purification, theatrical structures from which the various rituals could be watched, numerous storerooms and workshops, archive rooms, baths, paved courtyards, monumental gateways, staircases to the upper floors and complex arrangements of corridors. The palace at Knossos, much of which has been reconstructed, gives a clear picture of Minoan architecture and occupies an area of 22,000 square metres. During this period, many fascinating country houses were built, and examples have been discovered at Ano Zakro, Nirou Hani, Amnisos, Tilisos, Archanes, Ayia

Triada and elsewhere. A clear picture of the tightly-organised Late Palace-period settlements is to be gained from the finds yielded by the sites at Zakro, Palaikastro, Petra (Siteia), Gournia and on the islet of Pseira. In the Late Palace period, Crete reached the height of its power, dominating the entire Mediterranean (the Minoan thalassocracy). This development is plain in the art of the Minoans, which is best seen in the archaeological museum of Herakleio, one of the finest collections in Greece. There are also museums at Chania, Rethymno, Archanes, Ayios Nikolaos, Ierapetra and Siteia. Minoan art is notable for a powerful naturalist spirit, for its free use of colour and for its emphasis on scenes from ordinary life and religious ceremonies.

The wall-paintings found in the palaces and villas are outstanding examples of the artistic concerns of the age. In the Late Palace period, the Minoans used Linear A script, which has not yet been deciphered.

Around 1450 BC, most of the palaces were destroyed, in circumstances of which we do not know the details, while in 1400-1375 BC the palace of Knossos was burned down. In the next period of Cretan history (the Post-Palace period, 1400-1100 BC), the Myceneans of mainland Greece dominated the island, but they in turn came under the influence of Minoan culture.

The Geometric period saw the emergence of the city-states of Doric Crete (Aptera, Eleftheria, Gortyna, Phaestos, Knossos, Driros, Lato,

Itanos, Siteia and others), which followed the model of the Spartan system of government. In 69 BC the island was occupied by Rome, inaugurating a period of peace and prosperity. In the second century AD, the Emperor Hadrian demonstrated his fondness for the island by causing magnificent buildings to be constructed in the chief towns. In 824, the Saracens detached the island from the Byzantine Empire, but Nicephorus Phocas liberated it in 961. After 1204, Crete was sold to the Venetians, and the Turks captured it in 1669. In 1898 the island declared its independence, and in 1913 it was united with Greece. During the Second World War, the battle of Crete took place on the island, which was a centre for resistance against the occupying forces.

Crete today is one of the most highly-developed tourist resorts in Greece, as a result not only of its wealth of history but also of its natural beauties and the individual features of the daily life and customs of its people. Apart from important archaeological sites and museums, the visitor today can also enjoy places of unique natural beauty (the Samaria Gorge, Frangokastello, Mt Psiloritis, the Kourtaliotiko Gorge, Preveli monastery, Mt Dikte, Matala, the palm forest at Vai, the Lasithi plateau), the picturesque mountain and coastal villages of Crete, some superb caves (Falassarna, Yerani, Melidoni, the Idaean Cave, Zoniana, Trapeza, the Diktaean Cave), historic monasteries (Tzangarola , Gonia, Preveli, Arkadi, Our Lady 'Kera', Toplou), and large towns (Chania, Rethymno, Herakleio, Ayios Nikolaos, Siteia), which themselves have plenty of sights and provide a picture of the island's history. Nor does Crete lack idyllic beaches, clear blue seas and isolated, deserted areas which somehow manage to fit in successfully with the ultra-modern tourist infrastructure of the island.

# Heraklion

**A. HERAKLION:** This district contains the capital of the island, Heraklion, and the most important centres of the Minoan civilization (Knossos, Phaistos). Heraklion was founded by the Arabs in 824; it was known as Handax because of the great-fortified ditch that surrounded it. Today, next to the old city with its Venetian walls (14th-17th c.) stands the modern town, with pleasant buildings, a sound layout plan and numerous landmarks.

Besides the Archaeological and Historical-Ethnographical Museum, one can visit the Town Hall, the Venetian Loggia, the churches of Agios Minas (19th c.) and Agios Titos, the basilica of Agios Markos and the Morosini Fountain (1628). Six kilometres south of Heraklion lies Knossos, the foremost centre of Minoan culture. It was here, in 1900, that the magnificent palace first built in 2000 BC was discovered. The finds from the excavations

are on display in the Heraklion museum. Other major archaeological sites, in the district include Phaistos, further south, with its palace and sanctuary; Gortyn, which flourished during the Hellenistic and Roman periods; Archanes; Vathypetro, where one of the grandest Minoan villas was brought to light along with examples of rare pottery; and Amnissos. East of Heraklion one comes to Mallia, a picturesque, traditional village,

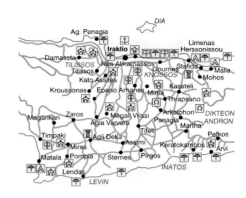

very popular among tourists. A Minoan palace-city was discovered here, while a little to the north lies the necropolis of Chrysolakkos. Viannos, a cave devoted to Minoan cult worship, was found near Arkalohori, and remains of the ancient city of Lyttos can be seen near the village of Xidas.

At Hersonissos, the port of Lyttos, there are ruins from the Hellenistic and Roman periods. Finally, one must not omit Tylissos, with its ruins of three Minoan villas, the inn of Niros with its Minoan megaron and the Labyrinth near Gortyn, a mazelike limestone quarry that has been linked with the myth of the Minotaur.

In addition to all this archaeological wealth,

*View of the world-famous beach at Matala.*

the district of Heraklion has no dearth of Byzantine monuments and beautiful scenery. It includes one of the most magnificent monasteries in Crete, that of Panayia (12th c.) at Kera Pediada. In the birthplace of El Greco, Fodele, besides the house where the great artist was born, one can also visit lovely Byzantine churches of the 11th and 12th century.

One of the most attractive areas in Crete, Agia Galini, lies on the borders of the districts of Heraklion and Rethymnon. Here there are wonderful beaches and enchanting grottos easily visited by boat.

Another delightful and famous beach is that of Matala to the south, near Tympaki, which has become an international tourist centre. The interest of its archaeological sites, its scenic beauty, its splendid beaches and the facilities it offers have made Heraklion one of the most frequented resort areas in Greece.

*Knossos: the north side of the main palace courtyard.*

# Rethymnon

**B. RETHYMNON:** The capital of the district, Rethymnon, occupies the site of the Minoan city. Rethymnon enjoyed its greatest prosperity during the Venetian occupation. The fortification walls and Venetian buildings of the older neighbourhoods date from this period. One of the most impressive mansions now houses the Archaeological Museum. Another landmark of the times is the small fortress of Fortezza, standing even today at the tip of the peninsula; it is closely linked with a number of local legends and traditions.

One of the most beautiful spots on the island (40 km. to the south) is Preveli Monastery, built amidst lush surroundings with an astonishing view of the Libyan Sea. Much closer to Rethymnon is the historic monastery of Arkadi, its twice-damaged church an impressive blend of baroque and local architecture. It acquired its present form in the 18th century.

The monastery was one of the main centres of anti-Turkish resistance. In 1866, the abbot Gabriel and his supporters blew up the monastery's gunpowder magazine, killing themselves and their enemies in preference to humiliating surrender.

Rethymnon is known for the many caves found in the area. The Yerani cave near the town, besides harbouring stunning stalactites, also contained remarkable finds from

the Palaeolithic and Archaic eras. One of the most important caves in Crete, and a centre of cult worship in antiquity, is at Melidoni, while the Idaion Cave on the Nida plateau is significant from the mythological point of view as the traditional birthplace of Zeus. At Zoniana there is still another cave, one of the largest on the island. Nor is the region lacking in archaeological interest. Ruins of the Classical and Roman periods at ancient Eleuthrna may be seen near Rethymnon. Although not considered one of the prime resort areas of Crete, the district has landscapes whose wild beauty is a delight, such as the Kourtliotiko Gorge, and wonderful beaches ideal for swimming and other water sports (Bali, Panormos, Preveli, Plaka, Ammoudi).

# Chania

**C. CHANIA:** The district of Chania, covering the westernmost part of the island, is the most impressive in terms of the diversity of its natural environment. It includes the White Mountains, the highest range in Crete, and one of the two largest plateaus, Omalos. The capital, Chania, lies in the northern portion of the district, where the ancient city of Kydonia once stood. For a while (1850), it was the capital of the entire island. The long years of Venetian domination have left their mark on Chania. Sections of Venetian fortification wall still stand in the old town which encircles the harbour, and there are numerous buildings from that era, such as the Rector's Palace and the Firca Fort. The Venetian church of San Francesco has been converted into the Archaeological Museum. Other sights worth noting are the mosques dating from the Turkish Occupation, the Historical

and Naval Museum, the Municipal Library and the home of Eleftherios Venizelos.

This part of Crete contains one of the natural wonders of Greece, the Samaria Gorge. Located in the western tip of the Omalos plateau (White Mountains), it is 18 kilometres long, 3 to 40 metres wide, with 600 metres its greatest depth.

Despite its difficulties, crowds of people hike down it every day during the season, winding

up at the village of Agia Roumeli with its pretty beach. From there one may take a caique to the other villages on the southern coast.

Midway down the gorge is another picturesque hamlet called Samaria.

Frangokastello, one of the most striking and best-preserved Venetian castles, lies in the eastern part of the district. Built by the Venetians in the 14th century, it has played a major role in local history ever since. Other places in the district also have interesting history. First comes Sfakia, on the south coast, with its attractive local architecture; its inhabitants have long been famous for their independent, rebellious natures and the town was always a core of resistance, no matter the conqueror. The Cretan Revolution of 1860 started in the village of Therissos, while Malema is famous as the site of the more recent Battle of Crete (1941).

Opposite Sfakia lies the islet of Gavdos, the southernmost piece of inhabited land in Europe. According to the myth, this is where Calypso enticed Odysseus and his sailors. From the archaeological standpoint, the village of Selli is of interest for its ruined ancient city and

acropolis, while the ancient city of Phalasarna near Platanos is also worth a visit. On the Gramvousa peninsula there are the ruins of yet another city of antiquity, Polyrrhenia.

The district also contains several noteworthy monasteries, such as Tzangarolon (17th c.), Our Lady of the Angels (16th c.) and Chrysoskalitis-sa. The Gonia monastery (17th c.) is also important, housing the Orthodox Academy of Crete. There are numerous charming seaside villages, especially on the northern coast, which is also more accessible. Worth visiting are Kolymbari, Platania, Palaiohora, Souyia and Loutro.

All the beaches can be reached by car except for Agia Roumeli and Loutro. Despite its popularity with tourists, the district of Chania is perhaps the most unspoiled in Crete, the most closely bound to the old customs and traditions.

# Lassithi

**D. LASSITHI:** Here one can find concentrated the most beautiful scenery in Crete. The centre of the district consists of the Lassithi Mountains (Dikti) and the Lassithi plateau with its characteristic windmills. The beaches and the little islands on the eastern coast have won international fame for their charm.

Agios Nikolaos, the capital and cosmopolitan resort, faces the Gulf of Mirabello, which takes its name from the Venetian castle on its shores. It is the site of one of the oldest churches on the island, the 9th century Agios Nikolaos. One should make a point of visiting the Archaeological Museum and the Salt Lake, Voulismeni, which is really the sunken crater of an extinct volcano.

To the north of the capital lie two of the most famous places in Crete, Elounda and Vai. The beach of Elounda with its super luxury hotel complexes attracts a host of cele-

brated guests. Here archaeologists have unearthed the ancient city of Olous. To the east of Elounda the landscape changes completely, culminating in the rocky peninsula of Spinalonga, a former place of exile, with a Venetian fortress at its tip. Two other spots of archaeological interest are located south of the capital – the ancient city of Lato, one of the most important in Crete, and the Minoan city of Gournia.

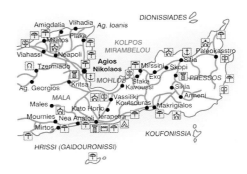

West of Agios Nikolaos (44 km.) sits Tzarmia-do, capital of the Lassithi plateau. In this mountainous region it is worth visiting the post-Byzantine monasteries of Vidiani and Kroustallenia. In the Trapeza and Diktaion caves objects of major archaeological importance have been found. Typical of the plateau are the countless windmills that adorn the area, whose side is split by the Havga gorge – an impressive sight.

One of the main towns to the east of Agios Nikolaos is Siteia, an important port and resort. From here one may visit the archaeological sites of Praisos, Itanos and Zakros, which have lovely beaches and green surroundings to offer in addition to their histori-

cal interest. This region also contains the Vai palm grove with its exotic beach which has become world famous.

In the southern part of the district there is another large town, Ierapetra. Built on the site of the ancient city, which flourished during the Roman era, it is today one of the main resort areas in the island. From here one may go to Myrto, a lovely coastal hamlet lying right beside its ancient namesake. At Makriyialo, another coastal village, there are ruins of a Minoan villa and the monastery of Agios Ioannis, while at Mochlos remains of yet another Minoan settlement have been discovered.

Lassithi has the best-known beaches in Crete (Vai, Elounda). But the whole island is worth seeing. Among the oldest inhabited places in Greece, it boasts the monuments of a major civilization, the Minoan, which has left its traces all over the island. Its mediaeval and Byzantine buildings also make a great impression on the visitor. The extraordinary scenic beauty attracts crowds of admirers and its modern towns offer all the amenities. Despite the island's popularity, Crete and the Cretans have lost nothing of their charm and originality.

*Windmills on the Lasithi plateau*

# THE ISLANDS OF THE
# IONIAN SEA

The Ionian islands (also known in Greek as the Eptanisa) are a group of seven islands in the Ionian Sea which extend along the coastline of Epirus, Sterea Ellada (Central Greece) and the Peloponnese with the exception of the island of Kythira which lies to the south of the Peloponnese, and which in administrative terms is part of the Prefecture of Piraeus. The Ionian Islands consist of Corfu, Cephallonia, Zakynthos (or Zante), Lefkada, Ithaki, Paxi and Kythira. These larger islands are surrounded by numerous smaller islands such as Othoni (the most eastern point of Greece), Mathraki and Erikoussa, all three northwest of Corfu, the Strofades to the south of Zakynthos, Antipaxi south of Paxi, Echinades and Atoko near Ithaki, Kalamos, Meganisi and Arkoudi southeast of Lefkada and Antikythira southeast of Kythira.

The history of the Ionian Islands is closely linked with their geographical position since these islands have always acted as a bridge between Greece and its contacts with the West. For this reason they were conquered on many occasions and were also fertile breeding grounds for the new ideas which reached Greece from abroad, both in ancient times and in more recent historical times. In antiquity, they were not part of a single political entity but instead each island had its own administration and form of government. In essence they were autonomous, and assisted the various Greek city-states depending on their political interests (see the historical data on each island separately).

During the Byzantine period the Ionian islands became part of the Byzantine Empire but frequently

broke away from it and were captured by foreign invaders, and in particular by the Franks. After 1204 they were shared out among rich Venetians who retained their dominance thanks to the support of their powerful armed forces. The sole exception was Corfu which became part of the Despotate of Epirus. When Constantinople was recaptured in 1261 the Ionian Islands were not liberated. In the years which followed each island was ruled at different time by Frankish lords such as Charles Anjou who captured Corfu in 1267.

In the 14th century, one after the other the islands fell under Venetian rule. It was then that they were placed under a single administrative structure for the first time. Venetian rule began in 1386 when Corfu was seized and continued with Zakynthos and Cephallonia (1500) and was completed with Lefkada in

1664. The Ionian Islands were assimilated into the Venetian state as a colony with the capital being Corfu. The form of government imposed on them was aristocratic. They were ruled by a Procurator General, who was commander of the Ionian Sea Fleet and each island has under the sway of local procurators who reported to special envoys of the Government.

The Venetians remained on the Ionian Islands until 1797 when the French Fleet captured Corfu and then the rest of the islands.

Between 1798 and 1799 the Ionian Islands were under the control of the Russians, starting with Kythira and ending with Corfu, which surrendered following the intense resistance to the joint siege by the Russians and Turks. In 1800 the Russians conceded the islands to the Turks creating the Ionian State, under the rule of the Sultan. A special Administrative Board was established on each island consisting of aristocrats. Under Turkish rule the people were deprived of political rights, a fact which led to an insurrection against the nobles. On Zakynthos, Cephallonia and Kythira there was an insurrectionary air and consequently a change in the political regime was proposed, but the High Porte did not consent. A new constitution was drawn up in 1803 abolishing the hereditary aristocracy and for the first time officially recognizing the Greek nationality and language of the residents of the Ionian Island Republic as it was called.

In 1807 the Ionian Islands passed into the hands of the French who took over administration of their acquisitions, carried out public works and bolstered education. Shortly thereafter came the turn of the English, whose domination began in 1809 on Zakynthos and was confirmed in 1814 with the conquest of Corfu following many, exhausting years of boycotting. At the Congress of Vienna held then, it was decided that the Ionian Islands would be free and independent but under

English protection. The first High Commissioner to the United States of the Ionian Islands was General Th. Maitland who was succeeded in 1824 by Fr. Adam. Many of the public works and measures taken to improve education were due to Fr. Adam. During the period of English rule there were major demonstrations by residents of the islands and bloody confrontations in the struggle for liberation. In 1863 England signed a Treaty in London recognizing the union of the Ionian Islands with Greece, to which they were finally conceded in May 1864.

Following their union with Greece the Ionian Islands gradually began to develop, primarily relying on agriculture thanks to their fertile soils. Even to this day their economy retains its traditional agricultural character, given that large parts of their terrain are covered with farms whose main products are olives and oil, grapes, wine and citrus fruits. Live stock farming and fisheries also occupy considerable numbers.

However, the largest growth area on the islands has been in the tourism sector. Beginning with Corfu – some decades ago now – all the islands both large and small, have attracted particularly large numbers of tourists from all over the world.

The Ionian Islands differ greatly from the typical Greek islands with their dry, barren soils. In most part they are fertile, giving a sense of abundance and vitality. Their residents are famed for their exuberance and are particularly sociable and love partying. These elements and the beautiful landscapes, deep blue seas, indented coastlines, rich vegetation, diverse traditional architectural forms and numerous monuments which stand as witness to their rich historical past, make them attractive both to foreign and Greek tourists alike all year round. Another factor contributing to this is their short distance from the mainland. Moreover, one can even

travel to Lefkada by road over a bridge that was recently constructed linking the island with the mainland. There are good connections to all the Ionian Islands both by boat and air.

Each island has its own distinct physiognomy, with unique sights to see. Cosmopolitan Corfu has its narrow lanes and multi-storey houses that remind one of Italian cities. Forested Cephallonia has its towering mountains and verdant Lefkada too is full of idyllic corners. Zakynthos was called the 'flower of the east" by the Venetians. Barren Ithaki is the symbol of goals and ideals, while the deserted Paxi are famed for their caves, vineyards and olive plantations and then there is Kythira, the island of Aphrodite, with its rocky coastline. Taken together they are real jewels not only of Greece but of the entire Mediterranean.

# Corfu

**HISTORY:** Known to the ancients under many names, the island owes its present name to the nymph Kerkyra. It has been inhabited since Paleolithic times, when it was still united to Epirus on the mainland, from whence the first settlers originated. Centuries later it was colonised by the Eretrians from Euboea in 755 BC and by the Corinthians in 734 BC. Subsequently, after winning independence, it became a great commercial power. Many rulers laid claim to the island and by 229 BC it was conquered by the Illyrians who in turn ceded it to the Romans. During the Middle Ages, Corfu was constantly raided by barbarians – the Vandals, the Goths and the Saracens in the 5th, 7th and 9th centuries respectively. In 1081 the Norman prince Robert Guiscard seized the island, but it returned to Byzantine rule until 1214 when it became a part of the

*Area:* 592 sq. km. *Population:* 92,261 *Capital:* Corfu (Kerkyra)
*How to get there:* By air from Athens and several European
capitals, by ship from Piraeus, Patras, Italy, Igoumenitsa, Paxos

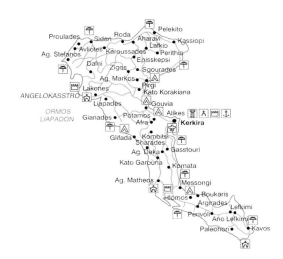

Duchy of Epirus. In 1267 it was taken over by
Charles d' Anjou and less than one hundred
years later the inhabitants appealed for aid
against pirate attacks from Venice, under
whose sovereignty they remained for
another four centuries.

Venetian rule has left an indelible imprint on
the physical appearance and social fabric of
the whole island. Napoleon's troops ousted
the Venetians in 1797, and in 1800 it became

the capital of the autonomous Septinsular Republic paying tribute to Turkey. The Ionians were restored to France seven years later and were recognised as a free state under the protection of England in 1815. The autocratic English administration stirred up the unionist spirit and the islands became part of Greece in 1864.

**SIGHTSEEING:** The prefecture of Corfu includes the Diapontia islands, Othoni, Matharaki and Errikousa, to the north and Paxos and Antipaxos to the south.

The capital offers entertainment possibilities, amenities and sightseeing for all tastes. It owes its unique grace and beauty to the four centuries of Venetian domination, symbolised first and foremost by the Old and New Forts. The Old Fort of Citadel built on a promontory jutting into the sea dates largely from the 16th century. Much of the city's architecture is Venetian in style; it has narrow cobbled streets (kandounia) and tall buildings with arches on the ground floor. A number of the buildings belong to the Venetian era – the Town Hall

(1663-1693) and the Bank of Greece (17th c.), among others. In the early 19th century the French engineer de Lesseps designed the Liston arcade on the Spianada, a replica of Paris's famous rue de Rivoli. Later the English built the Reading Society building (1836), the palace of St. Michael and St. George (1819), etc. The latter houses the Museum of Oriental Art. Other museums in the city include the Archaeological Museum and the Byzantine Museum.

Of the island's 800 churches, the most interesting are Agia Kerkyra (5th c.), Sts. Jason and Sossipater (10th or 12th c.) and St. Spyridon, the patron of the island. Four processions in his honour take place every year. Corfu's main ancient monument, the tomb of Menecrates, is in the Garitsa district, while the scant remains of the 6th century BC city are on the Palaiopolis peninsula, where evidence of the temples of Artemis, Apollo and Hera have been found.

Mon Repos, the former summer palace of the Greek royal family, lies on the outskirts of the city (no admission), while nearby there are the popular strolling places, Analipsi hill and Kanoni, overlooking the tiny monastery of Vlacherna and the much photographed Pontikonisi, Corfu's trademark.

The road to the north part of the island passes Kontokali and the bay of Gouvia, the lush resort areas of Dassia and Ypsos to arrive at

1. Kalami     4. Sidari     7. Couloura     10. Ypsos
2. Ag. Stefanos     5. Glifada     8. Paleokastritsa     11. Sidari
3. Ag. Gordios     6. Dassia     9. Kassiopi     12. Kalami

Kassiopi and Sidari, where Paleolithic artifacts have been discovered.

One can return via Agios Georgios, one of the island's most beautiful beaches, and Skripero.

At the tip of the south coast is the new resort of Kavos. To get there one drives through Maraitika and Benitses, two lively seaside villages. It is well worth making the detour to the Achillion in Gastouri, once the palace of the Empress Elizabeth of Austria and Kaiser Wilhelm, now a museum by day and casino by night.

To get to the west coast, the road leads first to Pelekas, a charming mountain village, a good place to view the sunset. The island's most famous beach, Palaiokastritsa, lies on the west coast, as do the resorts of Glyfada, Ai Gordi and many other delightful spots.

Corfu is a large, densely settled island, amply equipped to handle vast numbers of tourists. It is one of Greece's most popular destinations. Its geographic location, mild climate, lovely lush landscape – an endless expanse of every possible shade of green – made it a coveted prize amongst potential rulers until the last century and won it a wide number of admirers from ancient times up to the present.

# Ithaca

**HISTORY:** The traditional homeland of Homer's legendary hero, Odysseus, Ithaca has been inhabited since 3000 BC, though it only started to prosper around the first millennium and later. After the Roman era, it shared the fate of the other Ionian islands, becoming incorporated with the mainland state in 1864. The 1953 earthquake was one of the worst disasters ever suffered on the island.

**SIGHTSEEING:** Over the years excavations by the British School have revealed important finds, many of which are now in the British Museum.

On Mt. Aetos, Schliemann wrongly identified a sanctuary and ruined ancient acropolis as being Odysseys' palace; more recent excavations have since uncovered another acropolis at Plicate. Tradition maintains that the Cave of the Nymphs was used for the worship of the Naiads, while "Lois's' cave" held traces of a sanctuary and a great quantity of pottery from the Mycenaean to Roman eras. At Polis, which has retained its ancient name (City), ruins of the set-

*Area:* 96 sq. km. **Population:** 3,646 **Capital:** Ithaca (or Vathy)
**How to get there:** By boat from Patras, Astakos,
Cephalonia, Lefkada

tlement believed to have existed here have yet
to be found. The delightful capital possesses an
archaeological museum and a cultural centre.
Ithaca abounds with small, picturesque villages
(Stavros, Fries, Exotic, Kino), tiny bays and lovely
beaches, accessible by car, and a tranquil environment. With few hotels, Ithaca has not been
developed for tourism, but its rich past and dra-
matic scenery are attracting ever-growing
numbers of visitors.

# Lefkada Meganissi

**HISTORY:** Settled since the Neolithic era, Lefkada is identified by some scholars as Homer's Ithaca. It was colonised by the Corinthians in the 7th century BC and took part in the Peloponnesian War. Later conquered by the Macedonians, Pyrrhus (king of Epirus), and the Romans, it shared the fate of the neighbouring islands during the Middle Ages, and later succumbed to a succession of foreign rulers: the Italians, the Angevins (14th c.), the Turks (1479) and the Venetians (1684). It also saw a brief period of French supremacy (1797) followed by British domination (1815) before being united with Greece in 1864. Two major Greek poets were natives of Lefkada: Valaoritis and Sikelianos.

**SIGHTSEEING:** Lefkada, the capital, is a pretty town on the northeast coast of the island. It is separated from the mainland by a causeway watched over by the Venetian castle of Santa Maura (open to the public), originally built by the Orsinis in the 13th century. Places worth visiting are Lefkada's Italianate churches

*Area: 303 sq. km. **Population:** 19,947 **Capital:** Lefkada*
***How to get there:*** *By air via Aktion or by road through Aitoloakar-
nania, linked with Ithaca, Cephalonia and Meganisi by boat*

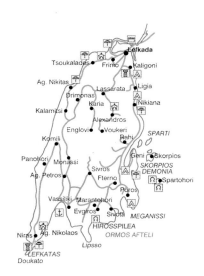

(Agios Minas, 1707; Agios Spyridon, Pantocra-
tor), and the Folk Museum, the Public Library
and the Archaeological Museum (in the same
building). Slightly outside of town to the
south there are two interesting monasteries,
Faneromeni and Virgin Megalovrisiotissa.

The drive south goes past Kalligoni, the
ancient capital with a ruined acropolis; Kari-
otes, Lygia, and Nikiana up to Nidri, the most
frequented spot on the island, second to the
capital. Nidri is a modern town with a pleasant
beach from which one can take a boat to the

offshore islands of Helonaki, Madouri, Skorpios (belonging to the Onassis family) and Meganissi. Across the harbour stands the peninsula of Agia Kyriaki with the church with the same name occupying the site of an ancient temple. Continuing south one comes to two of the most attractive beaches on the island, Poros and Vasiliki, and the enclosed bay of Syvota. The endless stretches of white sand on the west side of the island are even more impressive, at Agios Nikitas, Athani and all the way down to Cape Lefkata, also known as Sappho's Leap. The poet is said to have killed herself here – her example has been widely imitated since – near the now ruined temple of Apollo, one of the most important in the ancient world. The inland mountain villages of Karya and Eklouvi are also well worth a side trip.

Lefkada is equipped with tourist amenities and a good road network. A charming and lush island, with its share of historical monuments, it shares its quiet pleasures with a host of holiday-makers each year.

### MEGANISSI

Neighbouring Meganissi *(20 sq. km., pop: 1,339)* boasts the second largest sea cave in Greece, the famous Papanikolis grotto.

# Cephalonia

**HISTORY:** Excavations in Cephalonia show that the island was inhabited by 10,000 BC and that it particularly flourished from 1600 to 1000 BC. During the Classical period it was allied with Athens and later withstood the Macedonians, only to fall to the Romans in 187 BC. In the 13th century, it was ruled successively by the Francs, the Italians, the Turks (1484) and the Venetians (1500). The French took over in 1797 and were followed by the British in 1809. Like the other Ionian islands, it was united with Greece in 1864. The earthquake of 1953 devastated the island, except for the northern tip, and the capital Argostoli has been rebuilt over a larger area. Cephalonia has produced a great number of famous men in all walks of life (Coryialenios, Vallianos, etc.).

**SIGHTSEEING:** Cephalonia owes its curious shape and multiple natural phenomena to the predominance of limestone in its structure: the porous rock is easily eaten away. These natural phenomena include the famous "katavothres" (water mills), where the water disappears underground only to reappear mysteriously on

*Area:* 782 sq. km. *Population:* 27,649 *Capital:* Argostoli
*How to get there:* By air from Athens and Zakynthos,
by ferryboat from Patras, Kyllini, Astakos, Ithaca, Paxos,
Corfu, Lefkada, Zakynthos, Igoumenitsa and Italy

the other side of the island in the subterranean Melissani lake. Near Lixouri, Cephalonia's second city, a boulder called the Kounopetra (or moving stone) used to rock in the waves (since the earthquake the rock has stopped its strange behaviour and the water only trickles through the mills). Another strange and inexplicable phenomenon is the appearance of the harmless little snakes in the village of Markopoulo every August and their sudden disappearance after the 15th of the month. Argostoli has a small archaeological museum,

one of the finest libraries in Greece, the Corgiale-nios Library, and one of the most interesting museums in the country, the Corgialenios Histori-cal and Cultural Museum, showing what life was like in sophisticated Argostoli in the last century and before the earthquake. At Lixouri, separated from Argostoli by the Koutavos lagoon, the Iako-vatos Library is well worth a visit.

The island is divided into three parts: Krani, Pali and Sami. It has a good road network which connects its 365 villages – Assos, Fiscardo and Skala are among the most picturesque – with its three towns – Argostoli, Lixouri and Sami. Among the most interesting sights are Lake Melissani, the Venetian castle of St. George, the ruins of ancient Krani with their Cyclopean walls, the monastery of Agios Andreas, as well as the historical church in the village of Doma-ta. Near Sami there are the ruins of the ancient city of the same name; ancient Pali was outside Lixouri, near present-day Palaiokastro. From the hamlet of Haliotata one can visit the Drogarati cave, another natural wonder of Cephalonia. One of its chambers has such superb acoustics that concerts are often held here.

There are countless lovely beaches near Argos-toli, Poros and Assos, which combine comfort-able hotels, splendid scenery and a wealth of fascinating sights to attract numerous visitors seeking an interesting holiday.

# Zakynthos

**HISTORY:** In 1475 BC the son of the king of Phrygia, Zakynthos, conquered the island and gave it his name. Subsequently, Zakynthos changed hands constantly, passing from the Athenians to the Spartans, the Macedonians and the Romans. In 1185 it broke away from Byzantium and formed the Palatine Komiteia together with Cephalonia. Shortly thereafter it was taken over by the Orsini family (1204), falling to the Venetians in 1484, who held it until the French occupied the island in 1798. A brief moment of Russ-ian domination was succeeded by British rule until 1864. Since antiquity Zakynthos has been known for its admirable cultural development; its excellence in the arts continues to this day. Greece's national poet Dionysios Solomos was born in Zakynthos.

**SIGHTSEEING:** The 1953 earthquake virtually levelled the capital, which has since been rebuilt as it was, with impressive buildings and spacious piazzas. Worth visiting are the fine

*Area:* 402 sq. km. *Population:* 30,011 *Capital:* Zakynthos
*How to get there:* By air from Athens, by ferryboat from Kyllini
and Cephalonia, by bus from Athens via Kyllini

Post-Byzantine Museum, the Solomos Museum, the Public Library with its archives, the churches of Agios Dionysios (the island's patron) and Agios Nikolaos on the Quay. In the district of Bokhali above the town a massive Venetian fortress occupies the site of the ancient acropolis, while the church of the Virgin Chrysopighi contains a rare icon.

The interior of Zakynthos is dotted with charming villages like Maherado, where the famous icon screen in the church of Agia

Mavra can be seen, Maries, Othonies and the monastery of Virgin Spiliotissa (16th c), and Volimes, a mountain village with a number of interesting churches.

Laganas is the largest bay and the most popular beach on the island; it is lined with hotels, restaurants and bars. Other seaside villages with lovely beaches include Argasi, Vasilikos, Porto Roma, Alykes and Keri. Caiques are available for trips to the nearby islets of Plemonari, Agios Ioannis, Agios Nikolaos, Agios Sostis, Marathonisi, Pelouzo and the Strofades, as well as to the renowned Blue Caves.

An island with rich tradition, long history, a variety of natural landmarks and azure sea, Zakynthos possesses numerous modern hotels and rented rooms to provide its visitors with every comfort. For sports fans there are tennis courts, ping-pong tables, mini golf courses, sailing, water skiing, windsurfing, etc. Generally speaking, Zakynthos manages to combine an authentically Ionian atmosphere with the cosmopolitan environment of the big tourist centres.

# Paxos Antipaxos

**HISTORY:** A tiny island south of Corfu, Paxos has always been linked with its larger neighbour historically. It has been inhabited since antiquity, witnessed a succession of conquerors and remained for several centuries under Venetian rule.

**SIGHTSEEING:** Reminders of the Venetian domination exist in the ruined castle near the capital, Gaios. Built at what appears to be the end of a small fjord, its small houses are typically Ionian in style. Paxos is covered with olive trees and surrounded by wonderful beaches; this combination has long attracted summer visitors who have made their stay more permanent by building attractive holiday villas. The church of the Holy Apostles is worth a visit, as well as the three charming traditional villages of Lakka and Longos on the coast and Ozias in the

*Area: 25 sq. km. **Population:** 2,247 **Capital:** Gaios*
***How to get there:** By boat from Patras,
Corfu, Igoumenitsa, Parga*

inland. Not to be missed are the sea caves of all sizes on the west side of the island, which can easily be reached by small boat.

Antipaxos lies 3 nautical miles from Gaios. Its covers 5 sq. km. and has 126 inhabitants. From here one can take a boat trip to the two nearby islets of Exolitharo and Daskalio. Both Paxos and Antipaxos are green tranquil islands, perfect for a relaxing holiday.

# Kythera Antikythera, Elafonissos

**HISTORY:** Kythera, a large island opposite the southeast coast of the Peloponnese, was first settled in the second millennium BC by the Minoans, the Phoenicians and then the Mycenaeans. It belonged in turn to the Spartans, the Athenians, the Macedonians and the Byzantines, in later years, falling to the Venetians, the Turks and the British. Like the other Ionian islands, Kythera was joined to Greece in 1864.

**SIGHTSEEING:** In earliest times, Kythera was a holy place dedicated to Aphrodite, whose sanctuary lay near present-day Palaiokastro. Mycenaean tombs have been discovered at Palaiopolis, and the local museum's collection includes an important statue of Aphrodite with Eros. The capital is dominated by the Venetian castle (1316). Worth seeing are the Cave of Agia Sophia with its stalactites and stalagmites and Mylopotamos with its 24 water mills. Among the most interesting religious monuments are the church of the town's patron saint Elessa (1871) and the monastery of Virgin Myrtidiotissa (19th c.). An island of great natural beauty, Kythera has few